The impact of war on Sudbury
a Suffolk market town

NO GLORIOUS DEAD

Valerie Herbert & Shirley Smith

'Your monuments are lies

There are no glorious dead.

The dead stink and flies

Drink and befoul

The crimson tides of youth...'

Norman Bentley

Foreword
by Ronald Blythe

A strange and unanswerable sentiment attaches to war - any war. For us to question this sentiment, even after many years, is for some people questionable in itself. However, because we now understand what caused the two World Wars, the first precipitating the second, we see their victims less as heroes and more as humanity caught up in one of its inhuman moments. One of the clichés connected with the returning First World War soldier was that 'he never talked about it' - the terrible things he had seen, the dreadful things he may have done. But I have sometimes thought that this silence was born of ignorance for a vast number of those who fought in 'the Great War', and from every involved nation, could have had little idea of why they were there and what was happening, for they were virtually media free in a way which we can hardly comprehend. Both sides fought each other under a few religious and nationalistic texts and slogans.

When the Armistice came in 1918 - it actually means a pause not an end to the conflict - the death toll was so huge and the collapse of the old civilisation so shocking, that, in a sense, words failed both the victors and the defeated. In Britain the 'liturgy' of the Armistice Day service and that of the naming of the dead was created from many sources. Its literary basis is that of the Georgian poets and its memorials were unique in having every one of the 'the fallen' named on stone.

I began my book *The Age of Illusion*, published in 1963, with an account of the Burial of the Unknown Warrior in Westminster Abbey and of how this, then novel form of national shrine, came about. Edwin Lutyens had already carved the Cenotaph when the Vicar of Margate suggested that an anonymous body should be brought from the Western Front and buried in the Abbey. Other nations copied this tomb. The two minute silence originated in Cape Town. The words 'They shall grow not old as we that are left grow old' come from a poem by Laurence Binyon, a poet working at the British Museum. And thus was created the language and the symbolism of the official mourning of both World Wars.

It can offend us now. At the time, particularly between the wars when there was scarcely a home in the country without a lost son or father, there would have been some sense or nobility in it. But the faces have vanished. Millions have been killed by their own leaders in Europe, Russia and the Far East. To us the dead are not 'glorious' but tragic. And the Sudbury fallen, had they not been caught up in war, would have lived much as we have lived. My own reaction to the colossal tragedy of the First World War is terrible sadness mixed with anger against those who caused it and those who believed that a mile of ground was worth a thousand young lives. But it is an old story and each of us living now must try to understand it as best we can. It will become more and more difficult. This excellent book will help.

Ronald Blythe - 2009

Introduction

By the beginning of the 21st century memories and photographs of Sudbury men lost in the two World Wars were fast fading and in some instances had been totally lost, the long list of surnames and initials on the war memorial revealing nothing of their lives and deaths. This book sets out to tell the stories of many of these lost lives and to reflect the town, and the times, in which they were lived.

It all began when curiosity about a relative who died in World War I led to a mission by Royal British Legion member Shirley Smith, to collect the biographical material on as many as possible of the 301 dead from both World Wars named on Sudbury memorial. Painstakingly she searched official records, then contacted relatives by appealing in local newspapers and setting up a stand in the market place. Along the way she met her collaborator, retired journalist Valerie Herbert, who was similarly researching the lives of men named on the memorial in the church at the nearby village of Chilton.

Their early results generated huge interest at Sudbury History Society's biennial exhibition held in 2004. Town Councillor Nigel Bennett was among the enthusiasts, and in his subsequent year as Mayor he initiated a project to turn the much-enlarged research into a permanent memorial. The resulting tribute in text and photographs was unveiled in 2007 on large panels in the town's Heritage Centre and Museum. Funding came from an Awards for All lottery grant made to Sudbury and District Royal British Legion, which also financed an enhanced website version at www.sudburysuffolk.co.uk/photoarchive

This book is based on that project but has been greatly expanded to include more biographical material and to include the effect of the wars on Sudbury and its people. The result is a salutary reminder of the human and economic cost of war to a small market town. It also remembers with gratitude those who came back from the wars, many badly scarred by their experiences, as well as the families who mourned, and still mourn, both the lost lives and survivors who were permanently damaged. Neither this book nor the Heritage Centre tribute would have been possible without the support of these families. Many others have given generously of their time and knowledge, too many to acknowledge adequately, and we hope publication of this book will be some small recompense.

V. H.   *Sudbury 2009*

This map of Sudbury at the time of WWI graphically illustrates the impact it would have on the town. A war death would be mourned in almost every street and in some there would be many. Patriotism and a thirst for adventure led to men queuing to enlist in the early days but in 1916 conscription would be necessary to fill gaps in the trenches and launch fresh offensives. Altogether a total of 1,400 Sudbury men would go to war out of a population of just over 7,000.

Businesses would close for want of labour, others would struggle to survive. Life would never to be the same again and in 1918 the town would count the human cost. It would amount to one death for every six men who had gone to war. There would be empty chairs in homes all over the town and a pressing need to comfort and support mourning widows, orphans and parents as well as the disabled men who came home.

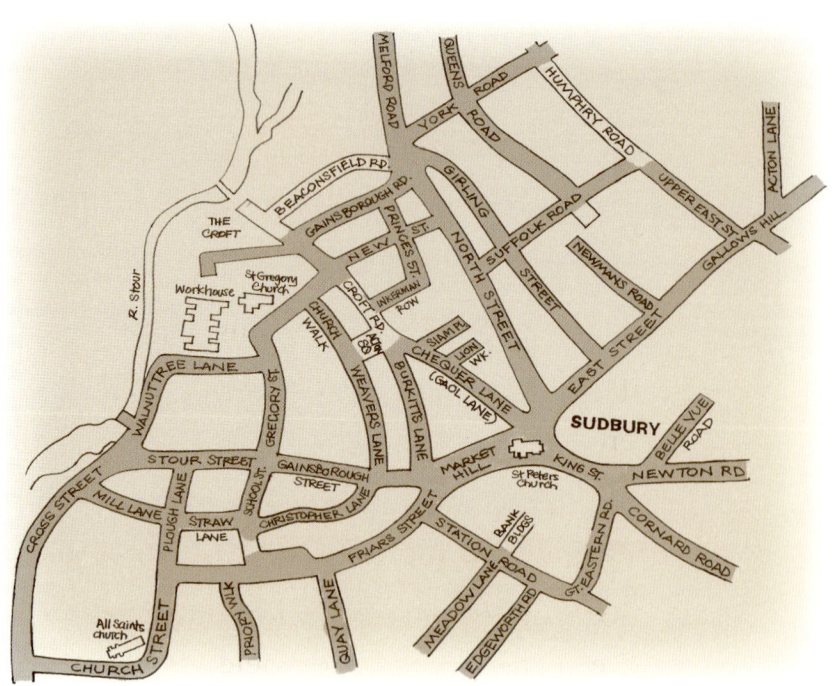

The pain of WWI: The dreaded telegrams reporting a death arrived in every street in the darker tint.

The town war memorial lists 241 names of those who died. Some families lost more than one son and nephews and cousins as well. The dead came from diverse backgrounds: employers and their employees, intellectuals and labourers, Boer War veterans and lads of 17 who enlisted by lying about their age. They served and died in 60 regiments, in the Royal Navy, and a few in the fledgling Royal Flying Corps.

According to national figures, more than twice as many were injured than the total killed, and long after the Armistice survivors were still returning home to Sudbury suffering from wounds and the effects of gassing, disease and trauma. Some listed on the memorial died after the war, many who survived were affected for the rest of their lives. With this level of casualties it is clear there could have been few living in the town who were not touched in some way by death or injury.

THE NATION'S GRIEF

+ One in every six families was bereaved

+ The war created 200,000 widows

+ 350,000 children lost their father

+ Two million British and Empire soldiers wounded

+ 240,000 amputees

+ Eight out of ten wounded returned to duty

Contents

World War One

		page
1914	Sudbury Territorials defend - horses go to war - the spy suspect - a 'Contemptible Little Army' - Christmas Truce letter	2
1915	The toll at Ypres - treating the wounded - disaster at Gallipoli - emigrants come back to fight - women join the war effort	11
1916	Death and heroism in a Zeppelin raid - the demand for 'cannon fodder' - slaughter on the Somme - fatalities at the railway station	28
1917	Six brothers in arms - a forgotten airship raid - death at sea - the horrors of Passchendaele - the hero denied a Victoria Cross	50
1918	The painful road to victory - a silent killer in the trenches - battles in the desert - the flu pandemic strikes - prisoners of war return	62
1919	Anguish and commemoration - 'pennies' for the dead - angry survivors organise - peace celebrations - the War Memorial story	72

World War Two

1939	A call to arms in Suffolk - Sudbury prepares to defend - gas masks, blackout and bomb shelters - the Polish Madonna mystery	84
1940	The 'miracle' of Dunkirk - lost in the Lancastria disaster - fear of invasion - Dad's Army keeps watch - Sudbury's radio hero	88
1941	Losses at sea and in the air - the sky watchers - women at war - a gun on the Market Hill - prisoners and wounded die together	95
1942	The 5th Suffolks captured at Singapore - Sudbury adopts a gunboat - deaths in Bomber Command - the toll among the boy sailors	98
1943	Drama over the North Sea - rationing bites harder - violent death in Sudbury - invitation to a pioneer flyer - the train takes the strain	104
1944	Sudbury welcomes the USAAF 486th - a bridge too far - the children's war - a love story in print - hush-hush royal visits - D-Day spectacle	110
1945	Sudbury celebrates peace in Europe - the terrible aftermath to Singapore - death on a Hell Ship - a fight for compensation - the story of Priscilla	126
1946/7	The struggle to win the peace - more rationing - fuel cuts - blizzards and floods - the banana story	136
	In memoriam : The men that Sudbury remembers	137

World War One

'As a tribunal for ascertaining the rights and wrongs of a dispute, war is crude, uncertain and costly'

David Lloyd George, Prime Minister 1916-1922

'The war to end all wars' 1914-1918

There was an immediate military response in Sudbury to the outbreak of the First World War in August 1914. The news was still passing around the town from mouth to mouth, when scores of uniformed men began to arrive at this building in Gainsborough Street.

They were the Territorial soldiers of D Company, 5th Battalion, The Suffolk Regiment, summoned to their drill hall headquarters to fulfil their obligation to defend Britain in time of war. It was an exciting prospect for men who mostly led humdrum lives on the land, in workshops and brick fields or serving behind shop counters. Most lived in Sudbury but more than 60 came from Long Melford and Bures.

Plans for mobilisation were so efficient that the whole battalion gathered at Bury St Edmunds that day, arriving in the evening at heights overlooking Harwich harbour, where they began constructing defences to protect the vulnerable East Coast from invasion.

It was hard work, but there were compensations - a sense of adventure, new surroundings, summer days in the countryside, comradeship and, for some, much better food. For D company the horrors of war were a year away and more than 3,000 miles away on the rugged barren peninsular called Gallipoli.

Territorial Force volunteers enlisted for four years to train for a defensive role on the home front in the event of war. They were paid an annual bounty on condition that they attended drills and summer camp. Training included target practice and signalling as well as gymnastics to increase their fitness. The Territorial Force was formed in 1908, replacing earlier militia that had a long history of support in Sudbury, and had fought in the Boer War. The 5th battalion of the Suffolk Regiment was recruited in West Suffolk, and the 4th Battalion in the east of the county.
In August 1914 the volunteers were ordered to report for full-time soldiering with greatcoat, haversack, spare socks and bootlaces, toilet articles, cutlery, clasp knife and sewing kit.

above:
The Drill Hall in Gainsborough Street, Sudbury

right:
5th Suffolks dig in at the coast

left : The 5th Suffolk Territorials parading in Gainsborough Street give an impression of how the massed influx of marching infantry must have looked in 1914. This parade in dress uniform was on the day of Edward VII's funeral in 1910

below : Working horses, like this pair harnessed to a Mauldon's brewery dray, were commandeered by the Army to pull Artillery guns in France

An army on the move...

Ten days into the war Sudbury was swamped by thousands of soldiers. Five thousand East Anglian Territorials from Essex and Suffolk marched through the town centre en route from Braintree to Bury St Edmunds in the morning. Then came Field Artillery, some bound for Waldingfield, Melford and Lavenham. When a halt was called, the line of stationary men and horses stretched from Ballingdon to North Street.

In the afternoon Herts and Essex infantry arrived hot and dusty after marching 16 miles in the August sun to be greeted in Ballingdon Street by flags and residents pressing apples into their eager hands, while in Church Street bakers handed out buns. Most were billeted in the town overnight.

Two weeks later the town welcomed men of the Leicestershire Yeomanry. They halted on the Croft where residents invited officers into their homes and provided a cask of beer for the men. Then People's Park was a night stop for 700 men and horses of the Staffordshire Yeomanry who had come from Bishop Stortford. This movement of troops was both part of their training and to distribute them to military depots around the country.

Horses go to war

WWI was the last major war that depended largely upon horse transport. Within days of the declaration the Army was busy in the Sudbury area commandeering hunters and heavier horses, the Suffolk Free Press reporting that some of the finest horseflesh in the neighbourhood had been taken by the Army for service in France.

Soldiers stopped vans and dogcarts to demand the horse, excuses were brushed aside and a set price paid. Among those requisitioned from Sudbury at that time were four from Oliver Brothers' brewery, and another belonging to Mr Mills of the Four Swans Hotel in North Street.

Huge numbers of horses were requisitioned for the cavalry, though warfare on the Western Front with its deep trenches, barbed wire and machine guns, eventually proved that the traditional cavalry charge was no longer a viable tactic. The greater need was for heavier horses able to pull guns and move supplies. Horses, like men, marched on their stomachs and Quay Lane became a focal point in Sudbury for preparing fodder for the Army. Horses suffered injury and deprivation along with the soldiers and an estimated eight million died during the war.

Ulmer 'the spy'

Within weeks of the outbreak of war gossip spread like wildfire that Mr Ulmer, the baker, had been arrested by police as a spy. The truth was that along with many thousands of German and Austrian aliens of

> Paranoia over the perceived threat of German spies in 1914 led to attacks on the businesses of perfectly innocent native Germans who had been naturalised. Even worse, there were cases of ordinary civilians being shot after failing to answer a challenge by soldiers guarding railway stations and public buildings. Paranoia led to a comical situation in Sudbury. The word spread that the Borough Surveyor had been arrested as a German spy and imprisoned. It transpired that the Council's water cart had been commandeered by the Army and the Borough Surveyor had been sending telegrams to sort out the problem. Somehow the surveyor was mistaken for the water cart!

military age he had been interned to reduce the risk of espionage and sabotage. Aliens were held in large camps, one on the Isle of Man holding 24,000 men.

Locals must have had some difficulty in giving credence to the gossip. German-born Fritz Ulmer, who everyone knew as Fred, was middle-aged and for at least 20 years had been a baker and confectioner in King Street, running the business with the help of his wife Edith who was a Suffolk woman from Eye. Their daughter Freda had been born in Sudbury and they sent her to a private school in Friars Street. Ulmer brewed ginger beer as a sideline selling it under his own name in glazed stoneware jugs.

Edith Ulmer carried on the business after her husband's arrest and it seems that she visited him in London. To their great sadness, their pretty, blonde daughter died of diphtheria in 1915 at the age of 15, and was buried in Sudbury cemetery. Epidemics of the diptheria killed many children before it was controlled by vaccination.

In 1917 Sudbury Justices fined Edith £2 for selling bread that was too fresh - she had contravened a new regulation banning the sale of bread until it had been out of the oven for at least 12 hours. At this time it was baked without preservatives and quickly

King street at the time of WWI. Fritz Ulmer's bakery is on the left with the smaller awning. The police station in the background is where Police Sergeant Thomas Reeder was stationed before he went to France with the British Expeditionary Force (BEF). He was 28, and a Company Sergeant Major in the Norfolk Regiment, when he was killed on the Somme in 1916. His wife Ellen and their two small children were living at the police station when they heard of his death.

went stale, and was then sold cheaply to the poor who relied on it as a staple food. The government hoped the regulation would reduce wheat consumption by making bread less palatable to the better-off who could afford alternatives. The regulation was introduced amid fears that the country was at risk of starvation since German U-boats were sinking one in four merchant ships on the Atlantic route. Food rationing was finally introduced the following year.

Not much more is known about the Ulmers except that Edith finally left Sudbury, perhaps to return to her native Eye. But then in 1921 an intriguing public notice in the Suffolk Free Press called on creditors of Gottlob Ulmer, an enemy subject, baker and confectioner of King Street, Sudbury, to apply to the Custodian under the Trading with the Enemy Act 1918, as the assets of his business were to be seized, realised and distributed.

Phyllis Felton of Sudbury Museum Trust with an Ulmer jug

Into battle with the 'Contemptible Little Army'

Five of the seven Sudbury men listed on Sudbury War Memorial who died in 1914 fought with the British Expeditionary Force of 80,000 hastily assembled from serving troops and reservists to help strengthen the French defences as the Kaiser's armies marched into Belgium.

The heavily-outnumbered British force surprised the Germans by its initial success at the Battle of Mons, but was then forced to retreat for lack of French support. The 2nd Suffolks fought a heroic rearguard action at Le Cateau, refusing to surrender until they were finally overwhelmed from the rear. Most of those still alive were taken prisoner, spending the rest of the war in captivit and returned from Germany in rags. Britain, France, Germany and their empires would fight for the next four years in the comparatively small area of Flanders and north east France which came to be known as the Western Front.

The Kaiser, who was a grandson of Queen Victoria, had ordered his well-prepared military machine to defeat Britain's contemptible little army, as he called the BEF, but it impressed German commanders and in the years to come the British survivors would proudly call themselves the 'Old Contemptibles'.

Had he lived Private Arthur Turner of the Coldstream Guards would have been among them but he died, aged 32, in November 1914, leaving his widow Jessie to mourn at home in School Street. He was a regular soldier who had fought in South Africa during the Boer War at the beginning of the century.

Private Harry Argent had only been out of uniform a few months after completing a nine-year engagement in the regular army, when he was recalled to the East Lancashire Regiment. He had no option but to quit his job at the Radiator Works in Cornard and go back into uniform. He was killed the same month, aged 29. Two of his brothers also served in France.

The first Sudbury man to win a medal went to France with the BEF. Private Clement Reginald Francis won the Distinguished Conduct Medal (DCM) but it was awarded posthumously. He was killed, aged 22, just before Christmas while attached to the 2nd Battalion, Suffolk Regiment. He had volunteered to carry a vital message 150 yards across dangerous open ground and was almost half way there when he was killed. The DCM was rated as second only to the Victoria Cross.

The rush to get into khaki

Such was the level of patriotic fervour early in the war that more than a million men voluntarily enlisted in the first five months. At times they queued at recruiting offices in their eagerness to get into uniform and 'teach the Hun a lesson'. At Christmas 1914 the Suffolk Free Press reported that military uniforms were much in evidence in Sudbury with a military guard on Ballingdon Bridge. Some soldiers in the streets and pubs might well have been 5th Suffolks home on leave, and the display of khaki could account for almost 50 men enlisting that week.

After their defence work on the East Coast, the 5th Suffolks had travelled by train to Brentwood in preparation for a long march through Essex, staying at towns and villages along the way. Their destination was the former Essex County Asylum at Mile End near Colchester. The location made them the butt of jokes but it was close enough to Sudbury to send home their washing and for their womenfolk to set about the tasks of sewing shirts and knitting socks for them.

Many troops went into action in WWI with minimal training, but that could not be said of the 5th Suffolks. Under the command of Lieutenant Colonel Morriss Armes, they trained for another six months before being shipped overseas. Even then they were ill-prepared for their first experience of action in scorching heat on the rocky terrain of deep gullies and thick gorse and cactus that awaited them at Gallipoli.

D Company's bugle boy Baden McMain was only 14 when he was called up with the rest of the 5th Suffolks. The boy from Girling Street was too young to go overseas so he served on the home front until he reached 18. He never did see action - he was waiting at Harwich to embark for France in 1918 when the guns fell silent. Baden was named after Colonel Robert Baden-Powell, the Boer War hero who defended Mafeking for 217 days and later founded the Scout movement. Baden was born the day the siege ended.

above: Fifth Suffolks with young McMain standing on the left.

The sinking of the 'Aboukir'

The first man on Sudbury's War Memorial to die in WWI is believed to be 21-year-old Able Seaman Harry Mumford. He went down with the cruiser *HMS Aboukir* in September 1914, dying in an action that altered the Royal Navy's perception of the threat posed by the previously underrated submarine.

In the space of an hour a lone German U-boat submarine despatched not only the *Aboukir* but her two sister ships *Hogue* and *Cressy* as they patrolled off the coast of Holland.

The first torpedo hit the 12,000 ton Aboukir under one of her magazines and she sank in 35 minutes after floating bottom up. *Hogue* and *Cressy* went to her rescue only to be torpedoed in turn as their boats picked up survivors.

In heavy seas a Lowestoft fishing vessel and Dutch trawlers joined in a rescue operation that saved more than 800 men, but 1,459 died, including young Mumford whose parents lived in Queens Road. The dramatic sudden loss of ships and men led to anti-submarine developments such as hydrophones to detect them under water and depth charges to blast them when submerged. But the heavy loss of merchant ships loaded with vital supplies continued until the risk was reduced by the widespread use of convoys with Royal Navy protection.

Germany hailed the sinking of the three cruisers as a great triumph and the Kaiser ordered the award of the Iron Cross, first class, to the U-boat commander Otto Weddigen. But such are the changeable winds of war that he died, along with his crew, a few months later while serving on a U-boat rammed and sunk by the British battleship *HMS Dreadnought*. He was 32 and newly married.

HMS Aboukir leaving Valletta Grand Harbour, Malta

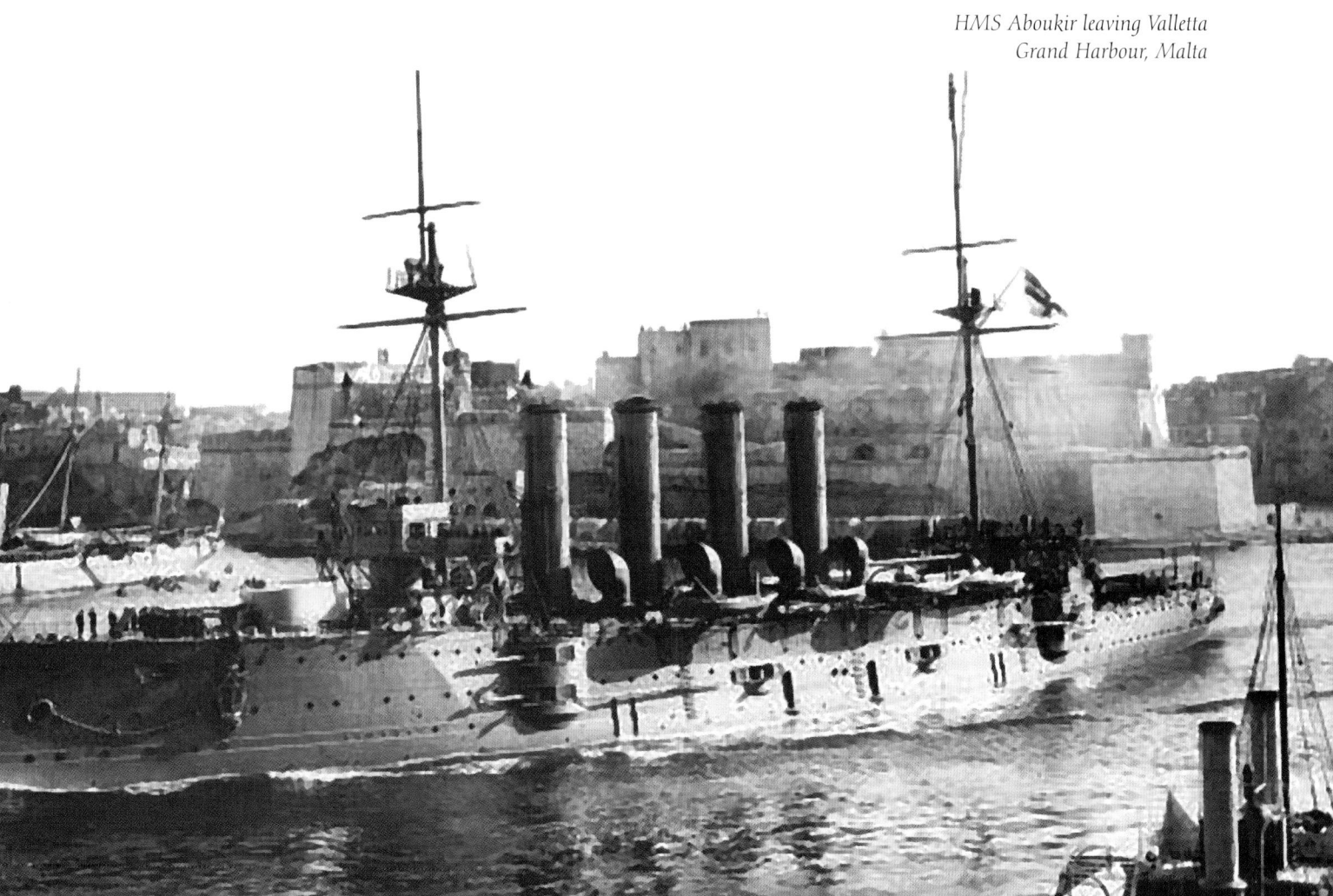

Sudbury's link with the Christmas Truce

One of the most remarkable episodes of the war was the Christmas Truce of 1914 when British and German infantry stopped fighting and spontaneously climbed out of their trenches and fraternised, an event later severely censured by British High Command on the grounds that such behaviour 'destroys the offensive spirit.' In other words, you need to hate the enemy not see him as your brother.

The inscription on a granite cross in Great Cornard churchyard (below) is minimal, but it marks the grave of a much-decorated soldier whose account of the Christmas Truce is regarded as one of the most graphic, and it is frequently quoted at Christmas gatherings in the English-speaking world.

This Christmas card was sent to Sudbury men away at the war in 1914, the Rector's greeting assuring them that they were among hundreds 'of whom we are so proud and for whose safe return we long and pray.' Regular attendance at church or chapel was part of life for many families at this time - there are the names of 21 members of the church on the war memorial board at Trinity United Reformed Church in School Street, and losses are recorded at other popular non-conformist churches in the town. Three fine, stained glass windows in St Gregory's Church commemorate those who died in WWI.

Lieut. Colonel Reginald John 'Jack' Armes buried there was a career soldier, one of the three Armes brothers from Sudbury who served in the war and the sole survivor. At 24 he fought in the Boer War as a lieutenant and was a captain at the time of the Christmas Truce. Promotion to a general staff officer followed and then staff officer with the Royal Flying Corps that lead to his appointment as Brigade Major at the headquarters of General Sir John French, the commander-in-chief of the British Expeditionary Force. Honours followed. The French appointed him a Chevalier of the Legion of Honour and the British made the now Lieutenant Colonel Armes, a Companion of the Order of St Michael and St George (CMG) in 1918. This was followed by the post of Deputy Director of the new Air Ministry. He spent his latter years living quietly at Brook House in Great Cornard apart from commanding the local Home Guard in WWII.

Jack Armes as a young man

His part in the Christmas Truce came to light during research for the memorial tribute to the town's war dead at Sudbury Heritage Centre. Before that, his letter describing the event had been wrongly attributed to his brother Raymond Armes who was killed fighting in the Middle East in 1916. The error is understandable, because in 1914 both brothers were captains in the North Staffordshire Regiment, only their second initial distinguishing between them.

The letter Jack Armes sent home to Sudbury describing his experiences on that Christmas Eve, reveals his pleasure and surprise but also his caution about the possible dangers and what the outcome might be.

The Captain's Christmas Letter

Somewhere in France   24 December 1914

Dear Beatrice

I have just been through one of the most extraordinary scenes imaginable. Tonight is Christmas Eve and I came up into the trenches this evening for my tour of duty. Firing was going on all the time the enemy's machine guns were hard at it firing at us.

Then at about seven the firing stopped. I was in my dugout reading a paper and the mail was being dished out. It was reported that the Germans had lighted their trenches all along our front and been calling to one another for some time – Christmas wishes and other things.

I went out and they shouted "no shooting" then somehow the scene became a peaceful one. All our men got out of the trenches and sat on the parapet and the Germans did the same and they talked to one another in English and broken English. I got to the top of the trench and talked German asking them to sing a German folk song which they did and then our men sang – quite well – and each side clapped and cheered the other.

I asked a German who sang a solo to sing one of Schumann's songs so he sang 'The Two Grenadiers' splendidly. Our men were a good audience and really enjoyed his singing.

Then Pope and I walked across and held a conversation with the German officer in command. One of his men introduced us properly, he asked my name and then presented me to his officer. I gave the latter permission to bury some German dead that were lying between us and we agreed to have no shooting until midnight tomorrow. We talked together, ten or more Germans gathered around. I was almost in their lines within a yard or so. We saluted each other, he thanked me for permission to bury his dead, and we fixed up how many men were to do it and that otherwise both sides must remain in their trenches. Then we wished one another a good night's rest and a happy Christmas and parted with a salute.

I got back to the trench. The Germans sang Die Wacht am Rhein a patriotic anthem, it sounded well. Then our men sang Christians Awake, it sounded so well. It was a curious scene, a lovely moonlit night and the German trenches with small lights on them and men on both sides gathered in groups on the parapets. At times we heard guns in the distance and an occasional rifle shot. I can hear them now in the distance but about us all was absolute quiet. I allowed one or two of the men to go out and meet a German or two half way. They exchanged cigars and smoked and talked.

The officer I spoke to, hoped we shall do the same on New Year's Day. I said, "Yes, if I am here". I felt I must sit down and write the story of this Christmas Eve. Of course, no precautions are relaxed but I think they mean to play the game. All the same, I think I shall be awake all night so as to be on the safe side. It is weird to think that tomorrow night we shall be hard at it again. If one gets through this show it will be a Christmas time to live in one's memory.

Jack

*The identity of Beatrice, the recipient of the letter, is not known, but she might have been Beatrice Whorlow, sister of draper Robert Sizer Joy who was killed the following year fighting with the Anzacs at Gallipoli. The two families were friendly and Beatrice and the Armes family were at one time neighbours in Stour Street. Jack Armes was married but his wife's name was Eleanor and they divorced after the war. He remarried, but not to a Beatrice.

Agony at Ypres and Gallipoli 1915

Ypres reveals the true cost of war

The ordinary soldiers called it Wipers; history knows it as Ypres, the ancient Belgian town that became the focal point of an area fought over for much of the First World War at the cost of many hundreds of thousands of lives.

Altogether 45 Sudbury men were killed or fatally wounded in the three great battles in the Ypres salient. The German Imperial Army launched the first in 1914 in an attempt to reach the Channel coast and then sweep into France on the way to Paris. The German second offensive in the Spring of 1915 was intended to break through the Allies' defences to capture Ypres, with its strategically important crossroads, canal and rail head. In an attempt to break the German stranglehold, the Allies initiated the third Battle of Ypres in the summer of 1917. Losses were so great that the name of the battle is fixed in the memory of generations as Passchendaele which was the final engagement.

The same terrain was fought over again and again, turning it into a nightmarish landscape of shell holes, barbed wire, shattered tree trunks and deep mud slashed by trenches, while Ypres and surrounding villages were shelled and bombed out of existence. Throughout the war men were killed by random shellfire in what was called 'daily wastage,' but the death rate reached appalling levels in these major battles made up of a number of separate engagements.

The 1st and 2nd Battalions, Suffolk Regiment, of regular infantry had many Sudbury men in their ranks because of the town's strong military tradition evidenced by the impressive Drill Hall in Gainsborough Street built in 1881. When war broke out, the 1st Battalion was brought back from policing duties in Khartoum and the 2nd was serving at Curragh in Ireland.

The 2nd Battalion had already been in action near Mons when the 1st Battalion went into action in a front-line position at the Second Battle of Ypres, experiencing the terrors of chlorine gas which caused choking and temporary blindness. The battle began in late April and raged for a month, the battalion losing 400 men including at least six from Sudbury. More Sudbury men died fighting with other regiments. There was nothing outwardly remarkable about any of them, but their deaths helped to change the mood of idealism in the Sudbury of 1914, to

---

Sudbury heard heavy gunfire out at sea in the early months of the war when German warships shelled Great Yarmouth and the Yorkshire coastal towns of Scarborough, Hartlepool and Whitby. Shells fell harmlessly on the beach at Great Yarmouth but killed 130 civilians, and injured almost 600 more, in the Yorkshire coastal towns. Flushed with success, German battleships sailed in January 1915 to attack the British fishing fleet in the North Sea. But British naval intelligence had been forewarned and a squadron of the British Grand Fleet, including cruisers and destroyers from Harwich, made ready. More than 70 warships engaged in the Battle of Dogger Bank, ships of both fleets being badly damaged and the German Navy losing the armoured cruiser Blücher with more than 800 of her crew.

awareness that the war many had rather optimistically predicted would be 'over by Christmas,' was going to be a long, bloody business.

Church bells were ringing in Sudbury when Private Willie Brown walked to the station with his father and sister on his way to France and his death. His sister could never again bear to hear the bells because of her poignant memories of the last time she and her brother had been together.

Private Willie Brown, 25, was killed just before the main attack. He had joined the regular army after growing up in a family of eight, first in Girling Street and then East Street. His father, Henry Brown was a maltster, skilled in the craft of preparing malt for the brewing industry.

Lance Corporal Harry Lorkings from Church Street died of wounds four days after Willie Brown, and the remaining 1st Suffolks from Sudbury were killed in early May. Private Sidney Binks came from a family of mat weavers living in Straw Lane. Arthur Crick, aged 32 and married to Emily, died of wounds and Arthur French and Alfred Golding were two of the many thousands whose bodies lie in some unknown place.

Three months later the shock felt in Sudbury over the number of casualties at Ypres would be pushed into the background by the news from Gallipoli, but in the meantime many more of the dreaded telegrams arrived at homes in the town.

Among those living in dread of the official telegram must have been Sybil Davey, living with her two small children in Waldingfield Road, Sudbury. Her husband William Davey had resigned his post as the golf pro at the Newton Green Club, to exchange his clubs for a rifle with the 7th Suffolks. In June 1915 he wrote to the club committee from 'somewhere in France' and in return was sent a parcel of comforts. Three months later Sybil's worst fears were realised when her husband was killed in action at the age of 25 and buried in one of the smaller cemeteries in Belgium. The Golf Club appointed his brother Arthur to succeed him and he remained at Newton Green for the next 60 years.

above : A peaceful moment before the war for golf professional William Davey, his faithful Bess and a boy caddie

above: Nurses at Belle Vue and soldiers in their 'hospital blues' uniform

Treating the wounded from the battlefields

Wounded soldiers from France began arriving at Sudbury rail station in February 1915 bound for Belle Vue, a large Victorian house in Newton Road converted into one of the first Red Cross convalescent hospitals in the country. Winter was especially harsh in the trenches and most of those in an early batch were suffering from frost-bite.

Sick and wounded soldiers arrived regularly in groups of around 20, a mix of English, Welsh, Scots, Canadians and Australians, with various medical problems. Janet Smith, a volunteer nurse at Belle Vue, noted in her personal log that three quarters of a group admitted in July had wounds, another had been gassed, one was suffering from shell shock, another had a heart problem and two had been buried when trenches collapsed.

That autumn patients included a group of five 2nd Suffolks, all of them suffering from gunshot wounds.

The hospital treated patients with Trench Foot, a bacterial infection caused by standing for long periods in cold, muddy water, which affected more than 20,000 British troops in the first winter. Feet rotted and became gangrenous without treatment - there were horrific reports of men's toes falling off as they removed their boots. The Army tackled the problem by making officers responsible for ensuring their men regularly changed their socks after drying and greasing their feet. The Army also abandoned the tradition of wearing puttees, cloth bindings around the lower leg, which would have restricted circulation to swollen legs and feet.

Belle Vue, with its staff of devoted doctors and nurses, must have seemed near heaven for men who had endured shelling, mud, rats, lice and other rigours of life in the trenches. The medical officer, Dr Rowland Rix, was a local GP, a quiet, energetic man in his 30s, and his wife Margaret served as the Red Cross Commandant. In WWII one of their sons was to endure years of ill treatment as a prisoner of the Japanese.

The nursing staff was supported by Voluntary Aid Detachment (VAD) auxiliaries who were amateurs with some training, and distinguished by the Red Cross emblem on their aprons. They included Mrs Smylie, wife of the headmaster of Sudbury Grammar School, and Mrs Charles Tippet both of whom would become war widows. Others included the mistresses of Brundon Hall and Chilton Hall, and the wives and daughters of businessmen and tradesmen in the town.

The town supported the hospital and its patients generously by way of the voluntary work and gifts. An August Bank Holiday fete and auction at East House, the home of Dr John Sinclair Holden, Sudbury's Medical Officer of Health, raised over £800 for Belle Vue. The well-to-do gave antique furniture for the auction, some buying it

above : Red Cross medal awarded to Janet Laura Smith of Sudbury for more than 1,000 hours of unpaid voluntary work as an auxiliary nurse at Belle Vue hospital

below : Doctors and nurses at Belle Vue Red Cross Hospital: Medical officer, Dr Rowland Rix, sits extreme left next to his wife Margaret, the Red Cross Commandant

back, or for a penny you could have three shies at an image of the Kaiser. Soldier patients at Belle Vue made Japanese doll pincushions to sell, and one man took the third prize in the hat trimming competition.

The town provided entertainment for the men they affectionately called 'the Blue Boys' because of the colour of their hospital-issue uniforms, cricket matches against the Grammar School boys being a favourite for those close to recovery. Sadly, many of those treated at Belle Vue were sent back to the trenches to fight again. Eight out of ten men wounded in WWI returned to duty, mostly to the front line.

The mass of casualties from the battlefields entailed setting up a vast network of clearing stations and general hospitals in France, the seriously injured being sent back to Britain for further treatment and convalescence.

Almost 700 had passed through the hospital by March 1919 when Belle Vue changed its role from treating men in uniform to helping those who had been discharged but were still suffering from wounds or disease. Patients included men suffering from being gassed and others with malaria and bronchitis.

A hospital in France, June 1915

Under an ugly white-washed roof
The beds are standing in rows,
And the stretchers come in a ghastly stream,
For men are standing the blows;
There are splints and bandages and lint at hand,
With basins and surgeon's knife,
And doctors and nurses and orderlies
Are fighting their fight for life.
The shattered leg, or the shot-pierced chest,
And the gassed man's gasp for breath,
Are telling the story that's true and real
Of the fields where men face death.
For the men have come from the Front and fight,
From a stern, stern game on hand;
And women are doing their 'bit' as well,
For the sake of the dear Homeland.

S.M.Wheeler

Sudbury-born Army chaplain Reverend Stanley Wheeler penned this verse in a military hospital in France. He published it in a collection that reflects his experiences while serving with the infantry. The poetic clergyman was 28 when he went to war, the privileged youngest son of Frederick Wheeler, of Friars Street, four times Mayor of Sudbury and owner of one of the largest firms of timber merchants in East Anglia. Stanley Wheeler dedicated his publication to the girl he was to marry. They raised four children, and in the 1930s he was Rector of Stapleford in Hertfordshire.

left : *Pages from his war poems*

The Army sent men with serious injuries to hospitals around the country. Twenty-one-year-old James Leonard of the 5th Suffolks was nursed in a Sheffield hospital, dying there in July 1917.

Private Frederick Barber of the 5th Suffolks was nursed a long way from home at Burghley House in Lincolnshire, one of the many large country houses requisitioned for use as convalescent hospitals. The soldiers fed well on meat and eggs produced on the estate but despite the care Fred died, aged 20, just before Christmas 1914. As the Suffolks were still training in England at that time, the likely cause of his death was either disease or an accident. His parents, Walter and Sarah Barber of Cross Street, had their son buried in Sudbury cemetery. In the same cemetery lies Private Clarence Francis whose parents kept a grocery shop on the corner of Church Street and Cross Street. He died of wounds, aged 19, at the Lord Derby War Hospital, Warrington.

Ballingdon-born Able Seaman Walter Ward was nursed even further from home, dying in a hospital at Newport, Monmouthshire. The one-time Sudbury silk factory foreman was 36.

Lance Corporal Joseph Wilson, of the 7th Durham Light Infantry, wrote this verse in a nurse's autograph book while recovering at Belle Vue from a head wound. It gives insight into nursing at the hospital at that time.

Tommy is back for a lie in a bed,
To be patched up, petted, nursed and fed.
Safe for a time from the distant storm,
Berthed in a hospital snug and warm.
Sister has taken him under her wing
She's a white-capped, slender slip of a thing.
She has frank eyes and capable hands
And a job she thoroughly understands.
Sister is merry and fond of a chaff
But she knows when to pity and when to laugh.
She helps Tommy through with his bit of a pain
And makes him feel his old self again.
She washes and brushes and makes him smart
Till the sight of him gladdens her orderly heart.
Special favours she grants to none,
She loves and mothers them, every one
And parts with her boys with real regret.
They don't say much, but they won't forget.

A treasured souvenir of life at Belle Vue.

Gallipoli

1915

Winston Churchill's infamous failure — Gallipoli

A year after the 5th Suffolks mobilised at the Drill Hall in Sudbury, they went into action for the first time at Gallipoli, the badly-planned and executed military campaign of 1915 that cost half a million lives before it was abandoned.

Winston Churchill conceived the bold plan in his role as First Lord of the Admiralty. The intention was to put Turkey out of the war in Europe by capturing the rocky Gallipoli peninsular and disabling forts guarding the entrance to the Dardanelle Straits. This would have given access to Istanbul and passage through the Black Sea to supply Russia. The first stage was a heavy naval bombardment intended to weaken the defences before invasion, but it alerted the Turks to the Allies' intentions and they strengthened their forces.

The 5th Suffolks would be in the thick of it. Recruitment had brought the regiment up to battalion strength when it sailed from Liverpool in July 1915 aboard the former Cunard liner *Aquitania*. Among the 7,000 troops on board were the men of Sudbury's D Company who had volunteered for service overseas.

In command was Lieutenant Colonel (William) Morriss Armes, managing director of Sudbury's largest employer, the Armes mat and matting factory founded by his grandfather. He was in his early 40s, a rather austere figure with a reputation for being firm but fair, who had been the 5th Suffolks' commanding officer for four years. He was so popular that the battalion had petitioned for him to stay in post after he should have retired. Morriss Armes, as he was known, had always wanted a military career but his ambition had been thwarted by his father's comparatively early death leaving him in charge of the family business.

The mood on board the *Aquitania* was buoyant. 'Old man Turk may throw in the sponge before we get there,' Morriss Armes wrote optimistically to one of his sisters, but the name Gallipoli was to go down in history as a futile military disaster that led to Churchill's resignation.

Before the 5th Suffolks sailed for the Mediterranean, British, French, Australian and New Zealand troops had already suffered huge losses fighting Turkish defenders under the command of German officers. The invasion had started disastrously, with heavy losses in the landing craft and among survivors pinned down on beaches dominated by high cliffs. Incursions inland were made at the cost of many lives.

Discussions about abandoning the campaign were in progress even as the Suffolks sailed for Gallipoli, but the chosen beach in Suvla Bay was comparatively lightly defended when they went ashore with the 54th Division in early August. It enabled them to move inland onto a grassy plain surrounded by scrub-covered hills, their worst enemies being the searing heat, tormenting flies, and a serious shortage of water - the ration went down to as little as half a pint a day. But the horrors that made the name Gallipoli infamous soon followed, as fierce defence by the Turks combined with disease and exhaustion to fell the men who had gone to war with such patriotic fervour and optimism.

The 5th Suffolks go into battle against the Turks

Two days after Lieut. Col. Armes and his men landed at Suvla Bay, the 5th Suffolks directed an attack on Turkish-held heights to the east of the plain. Together with the 5th Norfolks and 8th Hampshires they advanced through destructive artillery and machine gun fire without artillery support. It was a real baptism of fire: 'none of us thought we would come out of it alive,' Private F Clarke wrote home, 'Our brigade captured about a thousand yards but with a temperature of about 110 degrees and very little water, and with shells bursting all around within inches of us, you may imagine we had a very hot time.'

An hour into the attack Morriss Armes was hit in the chest as he led his men forward armed with only a revolver. He stood up and was still urging his men forward when he was shot twice in the head. A man with him left to go for help and that was the last sighting of the Colonel. His body was never found, an initial report of 'missing in action' not being changed to 'killed in action' until the following year. One of his brothers and a nephew survived Gallipoli only to die the following year.

A letter of sympathy sent to the Armes family by Captain H M Lawrence, the battalion's adjutant, reveals something of conditions in the aftermath of the attack. He concludes: 'Please excuse my jumpy scrawl but being in a dugout dodging bursting shrapnel and snipers, and worrying about how to get water for the troops, is all against being able to express half of what one feels. The heat is terrific and dysentery is catching 90 out of 100 again.' He survived the war and unveiled Sudbury's War Memorial in 1921.

The 5th Suffolks withdrew to a fenced ditch that offered some cover from the barrage of shells and bullets and dug in. For three days after the assault they suffered from thirst and lack of shelter from the scorching sun, as well as enemy fire day and night, until finally being withdrawn to reserve trenches. There the Battalion counted the cost - 186 men killed and wounded, three missing and more than 150 sick, mostly suffering from dysentery. The dead included six officers, apart from Morriss Armes, officers being prime targets as they led assaults. The British swiftly responded by ordering insignia of rank to be removed from uniforms.

In the same action, 250 men and 16 officers of the 5th Norfolks charged into woodland and are widely held to have disappeared, but in fact some bodies were later found and a few had been taken prisoner. The incident was given a high profile because the casualties included men from the King's estate at Sandringham. The 5th Suffolks took part in other attacks, notably one on a hill which involved crossing a salt plain in full sight of the Turks on ridges surrounding it, resulting inevitably in heavy casualties. After that, the campaign settled into trench warfare with the 5th Suffolks' front line being the fenced ditch to which they had withdrawn after the initial attack in which Morriss Armes was last seen.

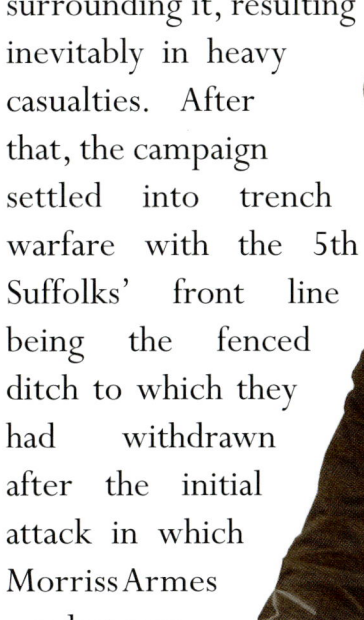

Lieutenant Colonel Morriss Armes

When memorial windows were dedicated in St Gregory's Church, Morriss Armes was described as a born soldier, recognised for his straightness, honesty and fairness. The congregation was told: 'Of all the men in this place who gladly and unwaveringly answered the call of duty, none was recognised so surely as doing the thing he loved best, and was envied in doing it, as Morriss Armes.' He was 43 when he died and had been praised for bringing the 5th Suffolks to a high state of efficiency even though he was apparently in poor health. He was not married and had been

aerial view of Chilton House

living with a brother, an unmarried sister and three servants at the imposing Chilton House, in Newton Road (above). It became Melford Rural District Council's offices and was demolished in the 1970s. It stood close to the entrance of Alexandra Road.

Report of Private Harvey of Hadleigh

'I was with Colonel Armes when he was hit in the chest on the right side. I dressed his wound which was a large skin wound. While I was doing this he was hit twice on the left side of the head near the eye by bullets that made small holes and blood came out of them. After this he stood up and called to some of the men. I told him to keep down, and I would go and try to get assistance. I could not find anybody, If I could have had help at first I would have tried to get him back but that was nearly impossible as the Turks were right on us. I had to wait till night to crawl back.' (It took him two days to get back to the Suffolks' lines).

Letter from Gallipoli

Morriss Armes' nephew, Lieutenant Harwood Clover, landed at Suvla Bay with the Royal Dublin Fusiliers three days before the 5th Suffolks. These extracts from a newsy letter sent to his parents reflect something of the 22-year-old officer's experiences.

'We have been fighting for six days and now we have two days rest. You will be pleased to hear that I got into the idea of shells and bullets bursting about me at once and have never suffered from nerves at all . . . the losses in our battalion are roughly 160 to date. Some battalions around us have been quite wiped out [a battalion was usually about 850 strong].

'I have no matches and no cigarettes and so hope to get some soon. It is chronically hot but very cold at night, and we have to sleep just as we are; no coats, blankets, body-belts or anything with us; we parted from them when we landed. I had my clothes off yesterday for the first time in six days, two lovely bathes [in the sea] and a change of underclothes. We average two hours rest a night in the trenches.

left : The hilt of Morriss Armes dress sword - given to Stour Valley Freemason's Lodge in 1919 and used in their ceremonial ever since.
right: Lieutenant Harwood Clover

The snipers are very numerous and get a good bag, I fear. They are the worst nuisance of any to deal with.'

Two months later, a letter sent home to Sudbury by Private Stanley Nunn, described the soldiers' monotonous diet at a time when the campaign had settled into trench warfare. 'Bacon and biscuits for breakfast, bully beef [corned beef] stew for dinner (with rice sometimes) and biscuits and jam for tea so you can see what our general diet is. We get so tired of it, but we get a little bread once a week.'

IN THE THICK OF IT AT GALLIPOLI.

Descriptive Account by Lieut. Clover.

Lieut. H. L. Clover has sent the following interesting letter to his parents:—

14th Aug. 1915.

We have been fighting for six days from last Saturday and are now having two days rest. You will have been sorely grieved to hear of our dear old Major—his death was instantaneous. Poor Julian was terribly wounded in the same attack. Harvey was wounded and 10 other men by shrapnel on the lighter coming from the ship to the beach. Altogether we had a very hot time at first. I am very fit and well, but have had many wonderful escapes. I had no idea of Charles Harvey's wound—we were on the same lighter and shrapnel were all round us, but at the time I thought we all escaped. You will be pleased to hear our Company, Battalion, and Division have earned high praise. Mac and I were the only officers left then, in C Company, after taking the hill on the Saturday evening. Now Capt. Palmer has come to us again—I am very pleased. I have only lost six men so far, mostly slight wounds. Poor McGrath, our C.Q.M.S., whom father remembers showed him our company's stores at Royal Barracks was killed in the attack about the same time as the Major (Tippet). The latter's death was a rifle bullet through the head. It has cast a terrible gloom over us, but out here one has to take things like this as philosophically as possible, and not allow oneself to get depressed.

Personally, you will be pleased to hear, I got into the idea of shells and bullets bursting about me at once and have never suffered from nerves at all. Now we walk about as if there wasn't a Turk in the place.

I cannot describe very much to you—I have no time at the moment—we are busy digging ourselves in on the side of a hill next the sea, and are for a bit only in general reserve. The losses in our Battalion are roughly 150 to date. Some Battalions round us have been quite wiped out. I heard from Uncle Morriss from Major Dixon yesterday. I was very surprised to see the latter. We are just behind Uncle's lot, who are having a bad time I fear. The Turks have just started shelling some reserves coming up; the shells whistle

Death of the Major

Among the early casualties of the Suvla Bay landings was young Clover's hero, the veteran soldier Major Charles Henry Tippet - Clover had even joined his hero's regiment, the Royal Dublin Fusiliers. The Major was killed leading an assault on a hill before the 5th Suffolks landed. A fellow officer reported: 'The attack was brilliantly successful, but before the top was reached our Major was shot through the head and his death was instantaneous. All the men loved him and he loved them. We have buried him where he fell and have placed a cross there to mark the spot.' He was possibly painting a rosy picture of the outcome of the attack.

At 52, Major Tippet was to old to enlist, but the War Officer accepted his offer to serve because of the acute shortage of experienced officers. In peacetime he had been a surveyor and land agent, living on the Croft with his family and playing an active part in Suffolk's political life as well as being agent for Sudbury's former MP, Sir Cuthbert Quilter. In a tribute Sir Cuthbert wrote: 'His death has caused a gap that will be hard to fill and in no place more than in Sudbury, where his cheery personality, his unfailing courtesy and his sterling worth endeared him to so many.' The Major

above : Major Charles Henry Tippett
left : Newspaper cutting of Harwood Clover's description of life at the front

was a keen golfer, playing a pivotal role in Newton village green becoming a golf course. He persuaded locals that it would not impinge on their ancient rights and would have advantages, such as money to be made through caddying. His achievement and personality made him the obvious choice for the club's first captain. He also took an enthusiastic part in Sudbury's social life and with his military bearing and good seat on a horse, he cut a dash as Sir Richard de Clare in Sudbury's 1911 pageant to celebrate the Coronation of George V.

His son, Captain Herbert Charles Tippet, served in his father's regiment, winning the Military Cross. He survived the war to become the second husband of Edith Shand, grandmother of Camilla, Duchess of Cornwall, and in that way has a tenuous connection with the Royal Family. The couple spent some years in the United States where he designed golf courses.

Loss of the Company Sergeant Major

After the disastrous first action at Suvla and other attacks, life became a matter of survival for 5th Suffolks as they endured artillery bombardments and almost constant sniper fire. In September the battalion lost Company Sergeant Major Wilfred Hunt, who was a key figure in the battalion and at the Armes factory. For 15 years he had served in the Sudbury Territorials and had worked his way up at the factory from clerk to manager.

'Without exception he was the best man in the battalion and his death has cast a deep gloom,' Captain Brian Oliver, commanding officer of D Company, wrote to Mrs Eleanor Hunt at her home in Cornard Road. 'We had been in the trenches for three days and were about to be relieved when the Turks started a rather severe artillery bombardment and heavy musketry fire all along the line. I was sitting in my dugout with your husband and my cousin, Captain C M Oliver, who was about to relieve us. We all rushed out to get into the fire trench . . . He [your husband] was standing close to my cousin when he was struck in the face, either by a piece of shell or a ricocheting bullet. It may be some comfort to you to know that he did not suffer as he was killed instantaneously. We buried him last night by moonlight.' Wilfred Hunt was 37.

Captain Colin Oliver was commanding officer of the Lavenham company of the 5th Suffolks, both and his cousin Brian ending the war with the rank of Lieutenant Colonel. They were descendants of brothers Edward and Henry Oliver who built the huge brewery in Cornard Road that was demolished in 1932, following a takeover by Greene King. Brian Oliver became joint managing director of Greene King and head brewer, while his cousin Colin Oliver returned to his profession as a barrister at law. His side of the family moved into farming and were in business as Boardman and Oliver, auctioneers, estate agents and charter surveyors with an office on Market Hill, Sudbury. The Oliver name still remains in Sudbury as auctioneers Sworders, incorporating Olivers, with premises in Burkitts Lane.

Treating the sick and wounded

The Army evacuated casualties from Gallipoli to Malta and Egypt. Infected wounds and debilitating diseases such as dysentery added many to the final death toll in this era before the advent of antibiotics.

Among the hospital deaths on Malta was that of Robert Dixon, who was managing this ironmonger's shop in King Street (below) when it was photographed in about 1900. By the time he was serving in the Army Service Corps as Major Robert Dixon, he owned the business in partnership with his former assistant William Scott. The name Dixon, Scott remained on the fascia for many years after his death. The Major must have been one of the oldest casualties of the campaign, dying at the age of 60 from what was recorded as exhaustion. He was buried on the island.

Sergeant David Pettit of the 5th Suffolks died of his wounds in Alexandria. He was 23, and the son of millwright Robert Pettit and his wife Anne, living in Station Road. Dysentery led to the death of Sapper Frederick Beer of the Royal Engineers who died, aged 21, in hospital in Egypt. Less than a year earlier he had married his sweetheart Ellen Crisswell and was a proud father. His widow married again but her new husband Fred Watton went to France with the Royal Engineers and is believed to have died two months after the Armistice. He might well have been a victim of the flu pandemic rife at that time. Fred Watton's mother was a Miss Beer before her marriage, so Ellen's two husbands might have been related.

Captured 'evidence' of massacre

The 5th Suffolks brought back from Gallipoli gruesome photographs believed to be evidence of a barbarous episode that was largely overshadowed by the war. The images of decapitated Armenian priests were confiscated from a captured Turkish officer by 20-year-old Thomas Portfleet.

They seem to be evidence of Turkey's policy of genocide against their mostly-Christian Armenian neighbours, on the pretext that the Armenians might side with Russia. The killing began early in 1915 with

far left: The Sergeant Major's death was witnessed by Captain Brian Oliver, right, and his cousin Captain Colin Oliver, left, pictured with Lt Col. Morriss Armes and battalion adjutant Captain H M Lawrence

the murder of 250 Armenian leaders and intellectuals, and the priests might have been among them. Later thousands of men, women and children were driven from their mountainous region into desert without food or water. How many died will never be known, estimates ranging from 500,000 to 1,500,000.

Tom Portfleet was a member of one of many bands of blood brothers who fought in the war. The five sons of Dutch-born Johannes Portfleet and his wife Clara living in Gregory Street, were all in uniform, three with the Suffolk Regiment. Before the war, three of the brothers had worked at Armes factory together with their father and sister. All but one came home from the war.

A soldier's memory of Gallipoli

'The bottom of the trench was springy like a mattress because of all the bodies underneath. The flies entered the trenches at night and lined them with a density which was like a moving cloth. We killed millions by slapping our spades along the trench wall but the next night it would be just as bad. We were all lousy and we couldn't stop shitting because we had caught dysentery. We wept, not because we were frightened but because we were so dirty.'

From *Akenfield: Portrait of an English Village* by Ronald Blythe, first published by the Penguin Press in 1969. The author was born in Sudbury and his father fought at Gallipoli with the 5th Suffolks.

The end of the campaign

The ill-fated Gallipoli campaign lasted for barely eight months before the evacuation of the surviving British, Australian, New Zealand and other Allied troops. As well as enemy fire, they had endured summer heat, with accompanying thirst, poor food and living with the stench of rotting bodies that lay unburied rather than risk losing more men to enemy gunfire.

At the end of September, heavy rainfall turned trenches into rivers and men drowned. Then frostbite and more deaths resulted from the biting north wind and heavy snow that followed. The 5th Suffolks had little protection, their gear having been already taken off the peninsular in preparation for a planned evacuation that was abandoned because of the severe weather. Frostbite became a serious problem and attackers and defenders suffered together. One trooper in the Suffolk Yeomanry was so badly affected by the frostbite that it was necessary to amputate both his feet.

The surviving 5th Suffolks were finally evacuated under cover of darkness in early December, in an operation that was for once a great success. In four months the battalion had suffered more than 800 casualties through death, wounds or sickness, and many of the 268 survivors shipped to Egypt were in a weak condition. Unbeknown to them, they faced the prospect of almost three more years of conflict with the Turks in the Middle East, in which they would lose many more men.

And, in fact, the Gallipoli survivors would not see home again until 1919 when they finally sailed home from Cairo.

> One of the most moving memorials to the dead of the Gallipoli campaign was raised by the Turks on the beach at Anzac Cove. It is inscribed with the words of Ataturk, the first president of Turkey, who as Mustafa Kemal fought in the campaign. It reads: 'You are now lying in the soil of a friendly country, therefore rest in peace. There is no difference between Johnnies [Allied soldiers] and the Memets [Turks] to us where they lie side by side in this country of ours… you, the mothers, who sent their sons from far away countries, wipe away your tears, your sons are now lying in our bosom and are at peace. Having lost their lives on this land they have become our sons as well.'

The emigrants who came back to fight in Europe's war

When Britain appealed to her Empire for military help in 1914, many thousands of young men who had emigrated in the late 19th and early 20th centuries volunteered to fight 'for King and country.' The names of ten who originated from Sudbury are on the town's war memorial.

Private Robert Sizer Joy had turned his back on the family drapery business on Market Hill, founded by his father - a former Mayor - to emigrate to Australia. He was 43 and working as a draper in Melbourne when Britain made the appeal and was so keen to enlist that he took five years off his age.

Eight months later, in April 1915, he was among more than 8,000 Australian infantrymen who died in the first stage of the disastrous Gallipoli campaign. He was last seen on the day his battalion landed on a heavily-defended beach surrounded by high cliffs, many in the invasion force having been killed by enemy fire before they even got ashore. Private Joy was with a party of 47 who became separated from comrades in the scrub and steep valleys. He was not among the seven who eventually struggled back to the Australian lines.

In 1920 his sister, Mrs Beatrice Whorlow, living in Cornard Road, Sudbury, was told that his body had been found and reburied in a British cemetery above Anzac Cove, as it came to be called in honour of the Australian and New Zealand troops who fought there. The name Joy remained over his father's shop on Market Hill into the 21st century until it became the men's outfitters Winch and Blatch.

Sudbury-born Wilfred Jennings sailed for Australia in the same year as Robert Joy, and as he was also a draper they might well have been friends. He was so desperate to join the infantry that he enlisted twice at different locations, being discharged as unfit on both occasions. He died of cancer in Brisbane the following year. He was 39 and had been in Australia for five years. He had given the name of his brother Frederick Jennings as his next-of-kin, and his address as the Freemason's Hotel in North Street.

Market Hill in about 1900 with draper R S Joy's shop nearest the camera on the right

> Private William Charles Carter was discharged as unfit only ten days after enlisting in Melbourne in August 1914. The 19-year-old groom told the recruiting sergeant he had served for 16 months in the Army Service Corps before leaving England. So far as the Australian Army is concerned, he then disappeared without trace. His name is on Sudbury War Memorial, probably submitted by his grandmother living in Inkerman Row, perhaps because she believed that he had been killed.

Another new Australian from Sudbury saw action in two wars. Private Lionel Foster landed at Gallipoli with the same Australian infantry battalion as the draper Robert Joy. When he volunteered he was farming and had been in Australia for only a year. Within a fortnight of the Anzac landings he took part in the Allies third attempt to capture the heavily-defended village of Krithia, in order to open a route to attack the forts guarding the Dardanelles. It was another costly failure, with a third of the attackers either killed or wounded. Among the dead was Lionel Foster. He was 33, and had fought in the Boer War was among eleven volunteers made Honorary Freemen of Sudbury for their patriotic service.

Canada was a big attraction for the adventurous. In 1900 it was offering free land grants of 100 acres in Manitoba and cheap land elsewhere. Two out of three of the first 30,000 men who volunteered for the Canadian Corps were emigrants from Britain, among them another draper Bernard Mattingly, who in 1904 had emigrated leaving behind an apparently comfortable life in Sudbury. His father, Robert Mattingly, owned the large men's outfitters store that once dominated the bottom of Market Hill, serving five terms as Mayor of the town and living in some style at Great Cornard, tended by three servants.

Why Bernard chose a new life in Canada is not clear, but family letters indicate that the six footer was something of a rebel, perhaps because he was the son of a second marriage and his much older brother was destined to inherit the business. Whatever his reasons, young Mattingly was a farmer and surveyor in Manitoba when he enlisted in the Winnipeg Rifles at the outbreak of war. The Governor General of Canada (the Duke of Connaught, a son of Queen Victoria) inspected the Canadian Expeditionary troops before they left for France and singled out Mattingly

above : Lionel Foster might well have been among these Boer War veterans parading on Market Hill

right : The Mattingly shop at the bottom of Market Hill photographed at about the time Bernard Mattingly emigrated to Canada

Canadian Memorial at Vimy Ridge

for praise, describing him as 'the finest physical specimen of a man in the ranks.'

He was fighting as a machine gunner with the Canadian Corps when it swept three divisions of the German 6th Army from dominant high ground to win the Battle of Vimy Ridge in April 1917. The tall new Canadian was killed in action shortly afterwards at the age of 31. His burial place is not known but he is remembered on the Canadian Memorial there.

Another emigrant named on the Sudbury Memorial is Corporal Arthur Jarmyn who had joined the Mounted Police in South Africa after a spell as a regular in the Scottish Rifles. When war broke out he returned to Sudbury to enlist in his old regiment, dying from wounds in July 1916 during the Battle of the Somme.

Together in death

The Cardy brothers seem to have done everything together. They served in the same regiment in the same the sector, dying only a day apart in August 1915 and now lie buried just 12 graves apart in the Cité Bonjean Military Cemetery in Northern France. It must have been a heartbreaking blow for their parents Maurice and Violet Cardy, who were living in London but had strong Sudbury roots. Their younger son Robert had moved back to Sudbury before enlisting in the Royal Fusiliers with his brother Maurice. The brothers were serving in the relatively quiet sector of Armentieres when they were killed.

Women do men's work

Thousands of women were working for the war effort by the end of the year, taking over men's jobs in factories and even driving trolley buses. By 1917 more than 200,000 women were working on the land to replace men in the Army.

The volunteers played a vital part in producing arms and ammunition, girls as young as 14 working 12-hour days, seven days a week in hot, noisy and sometimes dangerous conditions to meet the ever increasing demands of the Army. Some had previously been in domestic service, others had never worked before. Initially there was opposition from male employees, but a survey revealed that that in some factories the women's application and energy had more than doubled production.

The role women played in WWI spurred their demands for the vote.

Deaths in an airship raid and slaughter on the Somme

1916

Air raids by German Zeppelins killed more than 500 civilians in World War I, dropping bombs in areas as far apart as Tyneside and Kent as well as on London. The airships attacked at night creating terror as they cruised like silver ghosts above sleeping towns.

Sudbury has never forgotten the night of March 31, 1916, when the hum of engines alerted the population to a Zeppelin moving slowly overhead - speculation has it that the crew of L14 mistook glare from lime kilns for a factory. The four-engined giant dropped a mixture of high explosive and incendiary bombs in a string across the town, some exploding harmlessly but others causing five deaths.

Fifty-year-old Thomas Ambrose and his wife Ellen, 37, died in the wreckage of their home in East Street, so did their widowed next door neighbour Ellen Wheeler, who was 64. Damage was so severe that it was astonishing to see a teacup still hanging on its hook amid the devastation.

At the Horse and Groom pub next door, silk weaver John Smith, 50, had stayed on to finish his pint. It cost him his life, blast from the bomb catching him as he crossed the road to his home opposite. The fifth casualty, Rifleman Robert Valentine Wilson, 42, was taking a bath at his army billet on nearby Constitution Hill when another bomb exploded in the garden. He was badly cut by shards of flying glass and died as a patient in St Leonards hospital.

But for real heroism, another soldier also billeted in the town with the City of London Rifles could have been the sixth victim. Rifleman Bond was asleep at his billet in Melford Road when a Zeppelin incendiary crashed through the roof, setting his bed ablaze. His sergeant dashed into the house and carried the unconscious rifleman to safety before bravely returning to remove the bomb and put out the fire. The young rifleman survived and his rescuer, Sergeant Charles May, was recommended for the Distinguished Service Medal for saving his life 'at great personal danger to himself,' though the Army finally downgraded the award to a Military Medal.

Charlie May

Charlie May was badly affected by the smoke but recovered to fight in the trenches being promoted to company sergeant major and was finally commissioned from the ranks. After a successful business career he emigrated to America where he died at 72 from chronic respiratory problems that

above : Three died in these two houses in East Street
above right : Zeppelin bomb hero Sergeant Charlie May

1916

The night death came from the sky

were a legacy of being gassed in the trenches. His grandson, Dr Christopher May who is a diagnostic radiologist in Arizona, never heard him speak of the rescue, or of the war, except to say that he heartily hated it.

More targets for L14

Airship L14 dropped bombs at six locations in Essex on the night it attacked Sudbury including Braintree, Springfield (near Chelmsford), Stanford-le-Hope and Thames Haven on the river Thames. Five German naval airships took part in the raid which was intended to disable munitions factories in Eastern England. Airship L13 bombed Stowmarket, but failed to hit the munitions factory there, and L16 attacked Bury St Edmunds. Airships were often completely off course such as bombing Dover in mistake for Harwich. Even so, they left death and injury in their wake and caused fear among the population in general. The Zeppelin that bombed Sudbury was one of the German Navy's most successful, carrying out 17 raids on England and dropping more than 22,000kg of bombs. It was destroyed by its crew at the end of the war.

Fighting the Zeppelin raiders

Airships cruising at 50 miles an hour would now be a sitting duck but not in the early part of WWI as they were difficult to locate and flew high, making anti-aircraft fire largely ineffective even when aided by searchlights. Opposing them were Naval Air Service single-engine aircraft with open cockpits, from which pilots fired a variety of bullets and darts designed to penetrate the outer skin and ignite the escaping hydrogen gas as it mixed with oxygen. This ammunition included a bullet containing phosphorus which ignited on firing. This proved to be a hazard to the fighter pilots, since un-used bullets were so unstable they were liable to explode if the aircraft made a hard or crash landing. A number of pilots died as a result as well as from the Zeppelin's five machine guns. The raids decreased as the war progressed, newer and faster British aircraft proving more of a match for airships which were also vulnerable to bad weather. In reality the Zeppelin raids were more successful at damaging public morale than strategic targets.

Kapitanleutnant Aloys Böcker, commander of the Zeppelin that bombed Sudbury, survived the war. He came close to disaster five months after the raid when he crash-landed another airship at Great Wigborough near Colchester. It had been badly damaged by anti-aircraft fire and attacks by night fighters. Böcker and his crew survived, setting fire to the damaged airship before surrendering to a lone police constable. The Commander was later exchanged for a British officer held prisoner by the Germans.

above left : Local historian Tony Wheeler with a Zeppelin bomb
right : Böcker, the German captain
below : Skeleton of crashed Zeppelin at Wigborough

*The giant gas holders were a backdrop to the cricket ground
below : Gasworks staff in 1935*

Cut off the gas!

In the Spring of 1916, bombs raining down from the sky and causing death and damage were still a new experience in Britain and the Zeppelin raid terrified Sudbury. Earlier raids on the coast had left the country more indignant than alarmed and Sudbury had not considered itself a likely target.

In the aftermath of the raid, the local emergency committee ordered Sudbury gasworks to cut off the supply immediately it was warned of approaching enemy aircraft. This would have plunged almost the whole town into sudden darkness and the management resisted, arguing that with so many homes being lit by gas this would 'likely to give rise to very great dangers.' A compromise was reached, it being agreed that rather than cut off the supply the company would warn its customers of imminent danger by reducing gas pressure which would dim their lights.

The privately-owned Sudbury Gas and Coke Company had other problems. It had lost many of its workers to the Army including men with the skills and knowledge needed for the intricate process of producing gas and its by-products. On top of that, an order requiring all buildings to screen lights at night meant that stokers in the Retort House had to endure working with the ventilators and doors closed.

The gasworks finally closed in 1968 when the town switched to natural gas from the North Sea, after 132 years of using locally manufactured gas. Nonsuch Meadow and the housing estate at the far end of Meadow Lane were built on the gasworks site.

> Great grandfather Henry Keeble was not unduly troubled when blast from the East Street Zeppelin bomb shattered his bedroom window in Upper East Street. The 94-year-old told his family he thought the explosions were thunder since he had experienced worst storms when living in America. Henry lived to be 100 but one of his seven great grandchildren died fighting with the 5th Suffolks in the Middle East. In Melford Road, shopkeeper Edward Wheeler took a risk when a bomb landed behind his shop. He covered it with a bucket and sat on it!

Death of a local hero

Captain Raymond Armes was a hero in the eyes of Sudbury's young men. Not only had he played football for the county and captained a cup-winning Sudbury United team, but in his teens he had farmed in Nova Scotia and fought in the Boer War, which resulted in the whole of South Africa from Cape Town to modern Zambia being added to the British Empire.

There was truth in the account of him being captured by the Boers after his horse was shot under him. Three days later he had escaped from a wagon train in the confusion caused by a British shell falling into an ox team, though a bullet went through the fleshy part of his arm. But it was dysentery that finished his part in that war, and back home he settled into the community, working in the family mat-making business and in his spare time playing football, riding, cycling and running.

There was a sensitive side to him too, churchgoers knew him as assistant organist at the 15th century St Peter's Church on the Market Hill and he was a generous contributor to a fund to acquire the Lewis organ which is still a glory of the church. He sometimes played the organ at Foxearth parish church too.

The football hero was so popular that when he cycled to Bury to enlist at the outbreak of war, he took with him a group of young men equally bent on volunteering. Speedily promoted from the ranks to captain, he went to Gallipoli with the North Staffordshire Regiment and was evacuated after being disabled by heat stroke. His older brother was killed in another sector.

When the war against the Turks switched to the Middle East, Captain Armes was back in action but this time his luck ran out. He died during an unsuccessful attempt to reach 9,000 British and Indian troops besieged for four months by the Turks at Kut, south east of Baghdad. It appears that the Captain had just come out from England and was second in command of an assault when he was killed at the age of 37. 'He is a very great loss to the regiment,' his commanding officer wrote to the Captain's remaining brother. 'He was always anxious to do all he could for others.'

The besieged garrison of starving troops surrendered to the Turks after 143 days, many of them dying subsequently because of harsh treatment by their captors. Raymond Armes was buried on the battlefield in some unknown place, his name is inscribed, along with more than 40,000 others, on the British War Memorial near Basra, an area that would be fought over again in the 21st century. Until 1997 the memorial stood on the main quay of the naval dockyard on the Shatt-el-Arab just north of

above : British War Memorial, near Basra
left : Raymond Armes

Basra, then President Saddam Hussein had it moved at great expense to a less sensitive site 32 km along the road to Nasiriyah. The memorial is believed to have been damaged during the 2003 invasion of Iraq to remove the regime from power.

Captain Armes remembered Sudbury in his will, leaving £200 towards the upkeep of the organ at St Peter's.

Among the troops besieged at Kut was Gunner Frank Bridgman of the 86th Heavy Battery, Royal Garrison Artillery whose parents, William and Sarah Bridgman, lived in Station Road. He died, or was killed by enemy action, two months into the siege and was buried in the Kut War Cemetery. He was aged 29.

> The adventurous Raymond Armes was fascinated by flying and went joy riding around the Sudbury area in a biplane piloted by his friend George Bernard Ward, a former Sudbury Grammar School boy and eldest son of David Ward, owner of the Foxearth brewery. They were close friends, both serving in the same regiment, though Ward transferred to the Royal Flying Corps. George Ward was a squadron commander with the rank of major and had won the Military Cross by the time he was killed in France in 1917, his aircraft crashing following aerial combat.

Families at war

Some Sudbury families had many sons in uniform. The Suffolk Free Press reported that Ballingdon blacksmith William White and his wife Ellen had four sons in France. Only Sidney failed to return home having been killed in 1916 fighting in what is now Iraq. 'A very fine, well-mannered young fellow of excellent character, and a good soldier,' his commanding officer wrote to his parents. Fate apparently looked more kindly on Mr and Mrs Thomas Panton of Inkerman Row, which is now part of North Street car park. They had four sons and three sons-in-law in the services. None of their names are on the War Memorial.

Meeting the demand for 'cannon fodder'

Towards the end of 1915 the army was desperately in need of more recruits, partly to cover the huge losses at Gallipoli and Ypres, but also for the planned Somme offensive of the following year and a new battleground in Salonika. The euphoria of the first five months of the war when more than a million volunteered, had long since evaporated and enlistment had continued to fall despite the upper age limit for raw recruits having been twice increased from 30 to 35 and then to 40.

The solution was the Lord Derby Scheme which promised men of between 18 and 40 that if they registered they would not be called up until needed. In return they were given a khaki armlet bearing a royal crown to show their commitment and this gave some protection from taunts of cowardice. In fact single men who registered that autumn were called up as soon as the scheme came into operation in January 1916, followed by the first married men in April. The following month the Government introduced conscription making all men between 18 and 40 liable for military service.

Employers fight to keep men out of the army

Conscription accelerated the drain of manpower from farms, factories and other employment but individuals, or their employers, could apply to local tribunals for exemption or postponement. The tribunal of local worthies, sitting with an army representative, had to be convinced that it was in the national interest that a man continued his employment, education or training, or that conscription would cause serious hardship because of exceptional obligations whether it was financial, business or domestic.

Sudbury's tribunal sat frequently to hear applications both from the town and locality. With so many men already in the Services, employers were desperate for manpower. A representative of Dixon, Scott and Company, the ironmongers in King Street, won exemption for a 35-year-old skilled plumber with four children after telling the tribunal that half of his 18 employees were already in uniform.

The former Half Moon pub in Gregory Street

George Pilgrim, the 40-year-old landlord of the Half Moon in Gregory Street and the father of four children, was granted exemption on condition that he joined the Volunteer Training Corps, a forerunner of the Home Guard. His pub was demolished after WWII for road widening.

Dairyman Edward Byham of Ballingdon managed to retain an employee after complaining that one of his sons and another employee were already in uniform, and he faced the prospect of milking 18 cows on his own since his young son was terrified of them. The dairyman's eldest son, Leonard Byham, was killed in France the following year when a splinter from a bomb 'went right through his head.' He was 23 and mourned by his family, his young wife Winifred and fellow musicians in Sudbury Salvation Army Band.

In 1917 West Suffolk Education Committee gained exemption for Richard Gillingham, headmaster of Sudbury Grammar School, on condition that he stayed in his post. His predecessor had been killed in the Battle of the Somme.

In some cases tribunals granted respite for a few months, and from reports of hearings it is clear that members had sympathy for the plights of both employers and individuals. Grimwoods, the Sudbury builders, wanted six months exemption for a foreman working on an industrial contract at Long Melford, the tribunal gave them two months. Charles Death, a Ballingdon coal merchant, was given three months respite, and the same decision was made in the case of a foreman at Mauldon's Ballingdon brewery who was struggling to look after fourteen dray horses on his own.

Oliver Brothers' brewery lost two thirds of its employees to the war effort

Brewing and malting were important employers of labour in Sudbury, until the needs of the military made big inroads into their manpower. Before the war Oliver Brothers' brewery in Cornard Road had 50 employees and a stable full of horses for deliveries. In November 1917, thirty of their men were already in the Army when one of their two remaining draymen, received his call up papers. The brewery fought to get James Rowe exempted, pointing out their dire shortage of manpower and that 'it was not much good 'expecting a man of 41 to jump trenches.' The tribunal allowed the drayman to stay in his job until January in order to help the brewery cope with its Christmas trade. The father of three survived the war. The brewery did too, but it was taken over by Greene King in 1919 and the imposing building demolished in the early 1930s. Only the office on the Cornard Road survived into the 21st century.

From 'somewhere in France'

Contact with home was considered so important that the Army set up a huge organisation to handle letters and parcels. A soldier was allowed to send two letters a week postage free and delivery in either direction was seldom more than four days for those serving in France. Letters obviously took longer to reach more distant theatres of war, a soldier serving at Gallipoli wrote of mail taking two and half weeks Letters home were censored, both to prevent strategic information being revealed and to avoid negative news damaging public morale.

Farmers struggled to cope without the huge numbers of agricultural workers carried off by the war and this wartime scene in Sudbury shows soldiers deployed to help harvest the vast amount of fodder needed for its horses and mules. This group was probably being moved from farm to farm to bale and load hay when the traction engine paused for the photographer outside St John's Church in Girling Street. The military requisitioned all sorts of vehicles for the war effort, this traction engine belonging to Albert Rowe of Bulmer, who is wearing the collar and tie. It is believed that the woman standing on the steps of the mobile living accommodation behind the engine is his wife.

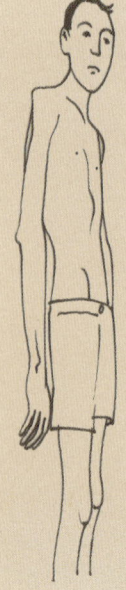

A weighty problem

The Army stretched the net in order to recruit men for service overseas. It formed 'bantam' battalions for those below the regulation minimum height of 160cm (5ft 3ins). From the story told by hairdresser George Challice, it appears that the military was even prepared to cheat in the drive for recruits. George was puny with a 76cm (30ins) chest and had previously been assessed as unfit for overseas service. The recruiting sergeant had other ideas, putting him back on the scales together with a 3.1kg (7lb) weight. It was a simple matter to then inflate his chest measurement by 5cm (two inches) to make him eligible for service overseas. There is no further record of him but he is not among those named on the War Memorial. Both volunteers and conscripts went to the war in poor physical condition resulting from poverty. Sudbury families with eight or more children to feed were not uncommon and tuberculosis was rife. Often it was the father who had the best diet, the argument being that he was the main breadwinner. In comparison, army recruits were well fed, sometimes for the first time in their lives. As a result there were reports of youths of 18 and older actually growing taller on army rations as well as putting on weight.

Lost in the Battle of Jutland

Royal Marine Isaac Felton died in the truly titanic Battle of Jutland in 1916 when 250 ships of the British and German fleets fought for supremacy of the North Sea. On 31 May the German High Seas Fleet met the Royal Navy's Grand Fleet about 100 miles west of Denmark. By the end of the following day 25 ships lay at the bottom of the North Sea along with 8,500 men. Lance Sergeant Isaac Felton from Sudbury and more than 1,260 others died that day when the battle cruiser *HMS Queen Mary* blew up after German shells detonated the magazines of two of her gun turrets. At the final roll call there were fewer than twenty survivors.

HMS Queen Mary, not to be confused with the liner *Queen Mary*, was the pride of the fleet and described at the time as the most beautiful ship in the Royal Navy. Commissioned only three years previously, she was armed with eight powerful 13.5in guns and the very latest in rangefinders.

The British suffered the greatest loss of ships and men in the battle, but the strength of the German Fleet had been seriously impaired allowing Britain to retain strategic control of the North Sea. This enabled the Royal Navy to maintain a blockade of German ports, starving the country of raw materials and food.

Lance Sergeant Felton was 38 and a regular soldier when he died. He had grown up as the son of a bricklayer's labourer and laundress living in Walnuttree Lane, enlisting in the Royal Marines at 18, bent on seeing more of the world than running errands on the streets of Sudbury. Two years later he saw plenty of excitement in China during the Boxer Revolution, in which that violent secret society set out to expel foreigners because of their increasing influence on China's trade and culture. Felton's ship put a landing force ashore, as part of a multi-national force that fought its way to Beijing to relieve foreign legations besieged by the Boxers for 55 days. The mission was successful though Isaac Felton was among the wounded. He recovered to continue sailing the world and had completed almost 21 years service when he was killed at Jutland. The Commander of the British Grand Fleet was Admiral (later Earl) Jellicoe, who in 1900 had been captain of Felton's ship *HMS Centurion* and was also injured in the Allied operation to relieve the legations in Beijing.

above : postcard of 'The most beautiful ship in the Royal Navy'
below : The moment when HMS Queen Mary exploded

Slaughter on the Somme 1916

The battlefields of Flanders and northern France claimed the blood of the majority of the Sudbury men lost in WWI, as it did in many communities. More than 30 of the men named on Sudbury War Memorial died in the first Battle of the Somme, a name that became almost a byword for slaughter. The scale of the joint Anglo French operation can be judged by the fact that the British Army sent 26 divisions into battle in a bid to take higher ground from which the Germans were dominating the terrain. The Suffolk Regiment alone contributed six battalions.

The battle began on July 1st, a day that proved to be the bloodiest in the history of the British army with almost 58,000 killed, missing or wounded. Almost 20,000 of these were finally listed as killed in action. They were mown down by machine gun fire and blown up by shells as they followed orders to walk calmly across no man's land. British commanders' confidence that the Germans had been severely weakened by a week-long barrage of shelling by more than 1,000 guns, was misplaced. Much of the wall of barbed wire in front of the German trenches had survived the bombardment and so had the enemy, having been largely protected by their deep and heavily fortified tunnels from which they emerged to exact retribution on a catastrophic scale in exchange for modest successes.

The Allies used huge resources of men and equipment to press forward, but the Germans resisted tenaciously and thousands more died in attacks and counter attacks. The battle lasted into November and only came to a halt when it became impossible to fight on in the deep mud and cold. The conflict had lasted for only five months but despite so much courage and sacrifice, the only territory gained by the Allies was a strip of land about 20 miles wide and six miles deep. The village of Thiepval, which was their objective, having been totally destroyed. Lance Corporal Harry Malyon, in his 30s, was one of three Sudbury men who were killed on that first terrible day. He was

Sudbury's 1906 cup winning football team. Harry Malyon is third from the right in the front row

The Battle of the Somme

This battle named after the river in Picardy, in north east France, raged for less than five months.

The estimated number of casualties varies but is usually accepted as: British 420,000; French 200,000 and in the region of 500,000 Germans.

married with two children and well known in Sudbury for his skill as a footballer having been a key player in Sudbury's 1906 cup-winning team. His parents, maltster George Malyon and his wife Jane living in North Street, had already lost a son in France, 24-year old Private Bert Malyon having died of wounds the previous year.

Another Sudbury loss on the first day was Private Leonard Sillett, 'as good a soldier as I had in my company, very hardworking, always cheerful and willing to do anything asked of him,' his Captain wrote to his parents, miller James Sillett and his wife Eliza living in Plough Lane. Three of their sons had gone to the trenches and he was the second to die, four months earlier they had lost 20-year-old Percy serving the 2nd Suffolks.

The third Sudbury man to die that day was Rifleman Harry Bond whose family lived in Ballingdon Street. The former weaver had been so severely frost bitten earlier in the war that it had taken a year for him to recover but he had then been ordered back to the trenches.

> Men on both sides suffered greatly in the battle, though Allied losses were far greater. German troops sheltering in deep tunnels survived the week-long bombardment of their lines before the Allies attacked on July 1st, but those holding trenches were frequently blown into fragments of flesh. Anyone out in the open bringing up supplies ran the same risk. One German infantryman waiting underground wrote: 'We are shut off from the rest of the world. Nothing comes to us. No letters. The English keep such a barrage on our approaches. It is terrible. Tomorrow evening it will be seven days since the bombardment began. We cannot hold out much longer, everything is shot to pieces.'

Death of the poetic school master

Those who fought and died in the first Battle of the Somme were largely volunteers who had enlisted on a wave of patriotism inspired by Lord Kitchener's poster appeal - Your Country Needs You. Among them was Captain Robert Stewart Smylie of the Royal Scots Fusiliers (below centre), whose usual uniform was his cap and gown as headmaster of Sudbury's Grammar School. He was 40 and married with three children when he volunteered at the outbreak of war, perhaps because so many of the boys he had taught were queuing at recruitment centres. Fourteen former grammar school boys are known to have died in the war.

Two weeks into the battle of the Somme he was killed by a bullet in the chest that went through his field pocket book. His commanding officer wrote to his wife in the often-used phrases: 'He was killed instantaneously while charging at the head of his company and setting a fine example of courage to his men.' The Imperial War Museum has the bullet-holed pocket book with his a plea in English, French and Latin for it to be returned in the event of his death to his wife living in the school house.

While serving at the Front he had written a verse for his two daughters and small son, that yearned for the day when the war would be over and they would be together. It was not to be and three more children had been orphaned.

Since I left you long ago, My three kids
There's a lot you'd like to know, my three kids
That has happened to your dad
In the varied luck he's had
In adventures good and bad, My three kids

I have ridden on a horse, my three kids
Captured from a German force, My three kids
And I've marched and crawled and run
Night and day in rain and sun
And shall do it till we've won, My three kids

And I'd rather be with you, My three kids
Yet you know I'm lucky too, My three kids
Lots of men I used to know
Now are killed or wounded, though
I remain, and back I'll go, To my three kids.

And when this long war is done
We shall have some glorious fun
Moll and Bids and little son, My three kids.

Captain Smylie's bullet-holed pocket book

The Major General's threat

In August Private Percy Partridge of Queens Road was reported missing while fighting with the 2nd Suffolks, his body was one of thousands that were never found or could not be identified. His wife inserted a advertisement in the Suffolk Free Press sadly asking for information, but without result. Percy was born in Bulmer when his father Alfred was an agricultural labourer and horseman, the family later moving to Ballingdon Street.

The 2nd Suffolks had been in action with the BEF since the beginning of the war despite having been almost wiped out fighting an heroic rearguard action at Le Cateau. The name of the battle would be added to those on their Colours, but their stand against overwhelming odds counted for nothing when the Battalion was ordered to attack yet again in mid-November.

The battalion adjutant described the conditions as incessant rain, trenches knee-deep in water, mud sucking men's boots off their feet, rifles caked with mud. Brigade headquarters was warned of certain failure in the impossible conditions, but the attack went ahead, the heavily-laden troops dragging their feet out of the mud and being slaughtered as they moved at a snail's pace. It was understandably a complete failure. There was no tolerance from the Major General commanding the Division. He told the 2nd Suffolks' Commanding Officer: 'The next time your battalion attacks, I shall put machine guns behind it and the men won't come back.' Among the 2nd Suffolks who did not come back in that November was George, son of horse keeper David and Sarah Parker living in Mill Lane. He was a regular soldier and had once served with the Suffolk Regiment on the tiny Channel Island of Alderney, which the British garrisoned for more than a century to dissuade the French from thoughts of invasion.

It was a case of being in the wrong place at the wrong time for Private Percy Hollingsworth, an orderly to a captain in the 9th Suffolks. He was killed by a shell as he waited outside a dugout for his officer. Percy came from a family of eight raised in a tiny cottage in Garden Row, his widowed mother supporting them by working in the tailoring trade. Percy and his brothers worked in the print trade and three sisters were corset and dress makers.

From school to the Somme

As headmaster of the Grammar School, Captain Smylie had appointed honours graduate Herbert Couch, to teach history, geography and modern languages. He did not join his headmaster at the recruiting office because he was supporting his ailing father, his stepmother and their three young children from his salary. Army pay for a private soldier was only a shilling a day.

The young schoolmaster was a victim of the 'white feather' treatment and taunts in the street, so the Derby scheme, enabling him to register his commitment to serve if needed, was some relief. But shortly after it became operational in January 1916 he was ordered to report to the 7th Battalion, Suffolk Regiment. Its destiny was the Somme.

Herbert Couch soon became a casualty, being shipped back for treatment at an Edinburgh hospital for a head wound caused by a shell that smashed his rifle. It was probably a serious injury as lesser wounds were treated at military hospitals in France. He recovered sufficiently to be sent back to the trenches but from letters home to his sister, it appears he was then injured again, this time a leg wound. In the summer of 1917 he was back at the Front again, writing home of longing to wash away his dirt and lice. Ten days later he sent a postcard telling his family he was quite well and would write at the first opportunity. He never did so. At 24, Private Couch died of wounds that same day at a casualty clearing station in France.

Portrait of Herbert Couch and Sudbury Grammar School as it would have looked when he taught there

Letters from the Somme

With good reason the customary letters sent to next-of-kin from a man's officer or NCO avoided gruesome and distressing details, but some provide insight into fighting at the Front.

After Private Ernest Cross was killed on the Somme, his sergeant wrote to his widow: 'Ernest was well in front of the advance and was doing splendid work when the first wave took a German trench. As the lads were going up this particular trench, a German officer came up from a dugout and shot your husband.' The former builder was 26 when he died fighting with the Royal Fusiliers.

Another Somme letter written to the parents of machine gunner Corporal William Matthews continued: 'We were holding the line just before the attack on Guillemont and the Germans counter attacked. Your son died like a hero at his gun, while the fire was still being kept up by the few remaining men of the gun team of which he was in command. The Germans shelled us very heavily indeed.' The young Corporal sang in the choir of St Peter's until he was claimed by the Army.

The life saving Bible

This pocket Bible probably saved the life of Private George Durrant by absorbing the impact of a bullet. His reprieve was short-lived, he was badly wounded by enemy shelling in July 1916 and died, aged 21, in one of the 11 hospitals established in Rouen to deal with the huge number of casualties from the battlefields. He was probably in the first Battle of the Somme as he served with the 7th Battalion, East Kent Regiment, which was there from the onset. His mother Sarah Durrant, living in of Ballingdon Street, Sudbury, treasured his Captain's letter which described him as 'a good soldier, always willing, bright and cheerful and faithful to his duty.' It continued, 'He was very popular with all his Company officers and all others in D [Company]. George tended his officer when he was wounded and stayed with him until he died then returned to his platoon. He died after a shell landed wounding him and several others.'

George Durrant's bible

The death toll rises

Thomas Stammers was well-known in and around Sudbury, driving the horse-drawn wagon used to distribute goods from his father's hardware and paint store in North Street. It was through his travels that he possibly met his wife May who taught at Assington school. They had three children by the time he was killed in early July fighting with the Royal Fusiliers on the Somme. He was 26 and is yet another whose name is on the Thiepval Memorial to those whose who have no known grave.

Thomas Stammers would surely have known railway goods clerk Charles Goody through collecting consignments from Sudbury station. Private Goody, of the 2nd Suffolks was killed in the same month. Living almost opposite the Goody family of ten in Station Road, Sudbury, were railway porter Tom Fish and his wife Jane. Their son, Drummer Edward Fish was in France with the same battalion and their sympathy for the Goody family must have been mixed with fear for their own son. A year later 29-year-old Edward Fish was mortally wounded.

Earlier in the year the Battalion had lost another Sudbury man when Private Harry Barber died of wounds. He has been mentioned in despatches to the pride of his parents, silk weaver Walter Barber and his wife Harriet, living in Newmans Road.

In August Private Charles Bayes, son of a Sudbury mat weaver, was killed instantly by a shell at the age of 33, his conduct had earned him promotion to a regimental policeman. He was killed behind the lines at a village which had a water point and billets for troops going to and from the front line. In the evening they would gather on the village green until the Germans found out and shelled it at that time of day. This might be an explanation for his violent death.

Deaths in September included that of Private Charles Poole fighting with the 24th Battalion, London Regiment. He was aged about 24 and had a sister working as a silk weaver. Their widowed father lived at Leprosy Cottage in Melford Road, named after the leprosy hospital founded there many centuries before.

The four Smith brothers were choristers at St Peter's Church on Market Hill when they posed for this photograph in 1907 but their proud parents, Arthur and Emily Smith, were to lose two of their sons on the Somme battlefield. Gilbert Claude, right, was killed in August, 1916, when he was 22. He had been in France for only six weeks. His older brother Arthur Angelo Smith, second from the left, died, aged 26, on the same battlefield in the Spring of 1918. Before the war Arthur had worked at Mauldon's White Horse brewery as a clerk. Both brothers are commemorated on memorials to those who have no known grave.

The four Smith brothers - choristers at St Peter's in 1907

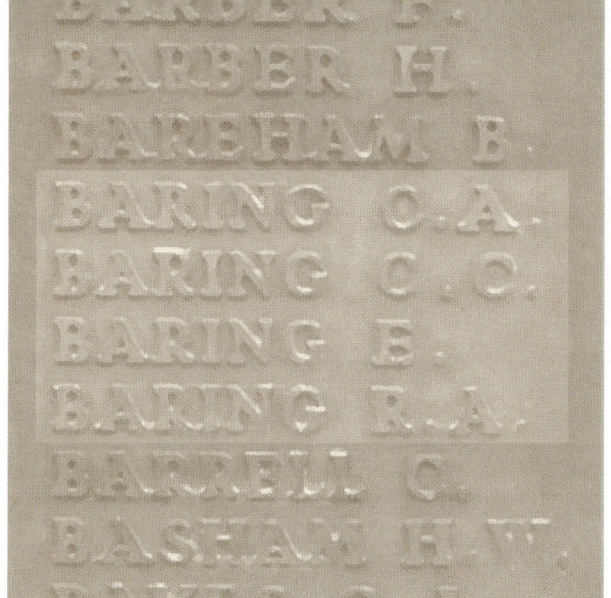

The mother who suffered the greatest loss in Sudbury was Amy Baring, a clergyman's widow living at Verne in Newton Road. Five of her sons went to war and four died fighting in France, the first on the Somme in 1916. Twenty-three-year-old Charles Baring was posted as 'missing' while fighting with the Australian infantry in September. Amy, like many in her situation, clung to the hope that he was still alive either as a prisoner or wounded in a hospital. The Australian Red Cross eventually located one of his comrades who had seen him fall during an attack.

The Baring brothers were offshoots of the Baring banking family and grandsons of a former Bishop of both Gloucester and Durham. Their father, Reverend Francis Baring, had served as a missionary in India and finally retired as rector of Fornham in north Suffolk. He was not to know the pain of losing four of his fine sons as he died shortly after the outbreak of war, the first of Amy's bereavements.

Charles and his older brother Ernest had emigrated to Australia as 15-year-olds to study agriculture at a New South Wales college. Both were farmers when they eagerly enlisted to help the 'Old Country' as did so many other young men making new lives in the Empire. Ernest Baring was killed seven months after his brother at the age of 27.

In the last year of the war Amy was to lose her two youngest sons. Second Lieutenant Cecil Christopher Baring was killed, aged 20, on the first day of the second Battle of the Somme in March 1918 - the German Spring Offensive. Less than three months later her youngest son, Second Lieutenant Reginald Arthur Baring died serving in France with the fledgling Royal Air Force. He was only 19. Amy lived on, dying in 1935 still mourning her sons. Two of them have no known grave, but all four are recorded on Sudbury War Memorial.

above : Amy's letter to the Australian Red Cross
above left : The Baring brothers' names on Sudbury War Memorial

Tanks roll into the battle

The Tank made its debut in the Battle of the Somme in September. Invented by the British, they caused panic in the German trenches as they lumbered across the battlefield at three miles an hour riding over craters and crashing through barbed wire defences. One took the village of Flers, the infantry following behind it rounded up prisoners.

The tank was a breakthrough in trench warfare but on this first occasion was not a great success. Of the fifty that should have gone into battle on September 15, a third became bogged down before it started. Tactics were ineffective and there were mechanical failures. In addition, the Mark I tank was difficult to steer and the four-man crews encased in steel had to cope with heat, noise and fumes generated by the engine. But it had proved the viability of a weapon that would play a major role in future wars.

The day of their first appearance on the battlefield is notable in military history, but it a was black day for Sudbury with three men killed, and another the following day. Private Henry William Gibbons died fighting with the 9th Norfolks near the village of Ginchy where tanks were used. He was 22 and his widowed mother Annie lived in Gregory Street. Another casualty was Rifleman Henry Sillitoe who was born in Sudbury but had an address in London when he died fighting with the King's Royal Rifle Corps. Rifleman Alfred Hills' parents Abel and Elizabeth lived at Coronation Villa in Queen's Road. Their son was married and living in Romford when he enlisted in the London Regiment. Private Robert Nunn was killed in action the following day, fighting with the 9th Suffolks at Flers-Courcelette where tanks were deployed. He came from a School Street family. Three of the Sudbury four have no known burial place and are commemorated on the Thiepval Memorial.

A broken down Mark 1 tank straddled across a British trench

photo courtesy Imperial War Museum IWM Q 002486

Bellringer Lee

Lance Corporal William Charles Lee, known as Charlie, was also among more than a million men of many nationalities who died during the Battle of Somme. He was killed, aged 23, a month before the offensive was abandoned after rain, sleet and snow had turned the battlefield into a frozen morass. Charlie Lee came from a hardworking Sudbury family; his father worked at Brundon Farm and the nearby mill; William at the town gasworks and his sister Daisy was a silk weaver. Father and son were regular bellringers at Sudbury's 15th century All Saints Church, taking part in a marathon peal of Grandsire Triples with 5,040 changes when Charlie was still a teenager. But when church bells rang out to celebrate the Armistice the Lee family was

Thiepval Memorial

in mourning, still not knowing where their son's body lay. Like thousands of others who died in battle, it is not known what happened to his body. Burial sites were obliterated in subsequent fighting, some men were blown to pieces, others disappeared into the mud. Bodies are still being found on the former battlefields. The names of these lost men from the first Battle of the Somme are recorded on the Thiepval Memorial which is the largest British war memorial in the world and visible for miles around. Standing near the village of Thiepval, it commemorates 72,000 Britons and South Africans who died in the Somme sector and have no known grave. Nine out of ten of these were lost in the 1916 battle that claimed so many Sudbury lives. The village was totally destroyed in the battle.

The Quaker who went to war

Members of the Society of Friends reject violence, which brings them into conflict with the Army in wartime, but the Wright family of well-known Sudbury Quakers had at least one son at the Front.

Robert Wright usually served behind the counter at his father's grocery shop on Market Hill, but was serving as a sergeant in the Honourable Artillery Company when he was killed in the Somme sector in late November 1916. He and his men were crawling back from the front line to a reserve trench when a star shell made them an easy target for enemy machine gunners. He was shot as he struggled to get an injured man to safety over ground pitted with shell holes. 'He died where he fell, performing the finest action an NCO could do, namely risking his life to try and save a wounded comrade' his Company Commander wrote to his parents, Edward and Sophia Wright who lived at Mayfield in Newton Road. Their son was 27 when he died.

The Wright family's shop on the Market Hill

Death at the Railway Station

There was more grief in Sudbury in the last weeks of the year. Tearful partings were commonplace at the railway station when men left to go back to the front, but none was more traumatic than on a December afternoon in 1916, when Private Herbert Theobald was being seen off on his way back to France by his wife, father and older brother. The three men had been drinking, perhaps to give young Theobald dutch courage as he might well have already fought in the first battle of the Somme. The scene at the station must have been heart-rending, with the young soldier kissing his wife and refusing to board the steam train and his family urging him to see sense. Finally he jumped aboard as it was leaving and in the confusion his older brother, Sgt. Major Thomas Theobald, and the ticket collector were dragged along between the train and platform. The Sgt. Major was already dead when his mangled body was recovered and the ticket collector died soon afterwards. The inquest jury recorded verdicts of accidental death and censured the young Theobald over 'the condition' he was in at the time. His death is not recorded on the War Memorial so apparently he survived to return to his home in Gregory Street.

Another Armes family loss

Just two days before Christmas 1916 the Armes family was in mourning for a third war death after Lieutenant Harwood Linay 'George' Clover, who wrote the newsy early letter from Gallipoli, died suddenly. He had been severely injured by a bomb just days after penning the letter to his parents, Sudbury mill owner Isaac Clover and his wife Alice who was a sister of the Armes brothers.

Surgeons considered amputating his shattered arm, but he recovered sufficiently over a period of a year to warrant a posting as acting adjutant to the Royal Flying Corps at Ripon. Two months later he was dead at 23 from meningitis, his injury considered to be a contributory factor. He was buried with full military honours at Sudbury cemetery and this stained glass window depicting St George slaying the dragon is his memorial in St Gregory's church. George Clover had been expected to take over the running of Sudbury Mill from his father but it passed to a cousin. George Clover's younger brother Rodney, opted for a career in the Royal Navy but eventually took over the Armes family business.

Sudbury station - scene of the two deaths

above : the Clover family home in Stour Street
below : stained glass in St Gregory's church

The cost of war to one family

This Victorian family portrait of the Armes family is an example of the extent to which WWI devastated some families. The death of Lieutenant Clover, pictured as a boy holding his grandmother's hand, was the third. When the Armes family posed in 1898, the widowed matriarch Sarah Armes was sitting proudly among her three handsome sons, her daughters, son-in-law and two grandsons. The family was respected and prosperous, living at Hardwicke House in Stour Street. Their business of making coir and sisal matting was a major employer in the town and the Armes dynasty seemed secure, with Morriss Armes, standing on the right, running the firm with the help of his brother Raymond who stands next to him.

War had changed the family's fortunes drastically by the end of 1916. Morriss Armes had been killed at Gallipoli and his brother Raymond, had died in the vain attempt to relieve the siege at Kut, the sudden death of their nephew 'George' Clover followed.

The family was already in mourning at the outbreak of war. Their youngest sister Kathleen, standing between them in the portrait, had died of diphtheria earlier in 1914, together with her young son. She was the wife of Reverend John James Jones, Rector of St Gregory's and St Peter's churches, they had married three years earlier. The third Armes brother, Reginald 'Jack' Armes, sitting on the right in the family group, was the only one to survive the war and his only son died young. He wrote the account of the Christmas Truce.

Sarah Armes did not live to see the tragedies as she died in 1910. Her grandson Rodney Clover (the baby in the photograph) eventually took over the family firm after a career in the Royal Navy. His mother Alice Armes was married to Sudbury mill owner Isaac Clover, who stands behind her.

The scale of lives lost in the war is so great it is not easy to envisage, but by the end of the war it would total eight million military deaths among the combatants of all the nations involved.

Blood, mud and tears

No end to the slaughter

When the New Year dawned in 1917 Britain entered its fourth year at war with no sign of an end to the killing and by the following Christmas the names of another 71 Sudbury men had been added to the town's losses. The cost of prosecuting the war was soaring too, the Government offering 30-year war loans at five per cent to help meet enormous debts. It would be the year when America came into the war and the Bolsheviks seized power in Russia enabling the Germans to move many divisions to the Western Front, but in Sudbury, as elsewhere, it was the dreaded War Office telegrams that had most impact on people's lives.

Six brothers in arms

On New Year's Day the Wheeler family lost the first of their two sons near Arras. A shell hit a party of 13 sent out to repair a trench blown up the night before. When the smoke cleared nine were dead or dying among them Frank Wheeler (left). 'They've got me this time,' he told a friend who went to help him, dying as he asked about an ambulance. He was 26 and had been in France for less than two months with the 75th Canadian Infantry Regiment. He had emigrated to Canada seeking a life with wider horizons and had volunteered to fight. On the day his parents heard of his death their youngest son Harry (right), left for France.

All six of Edward and Martha Wheeler's sons fought in the war. The Wheelers are an old Sudbury family, this branch originally owning furniture and grocery businesses in Melford Road. The couple had three sons, including Frank, by the time they moved to Lavenham where Edward Wheeler took over a butcher's shop and fathered three more boys.

Six months later Fred Wheeler, another of their sons born in Sudbury, was blown to pieces by a shell as he sheltered in a crater close to the German lines. Three out of every five casualties in WWI were caused by shellfire. Fred (right) was 31, married and the father of three children.

The remaining four brothers survived trench warfare, though one was wounded twice. The eldest, Ted Wheeler (right) closed his butcher's shop in North Street to join the colours and re-opened it after the war. The fifth son Alfred (left), was to lose one of his two sons in 1943 when the submarine *HMS Turbulent* was lost with all her crew in the Mediterranean. The Wheeler's remaining son Percy (right), also survived the war.

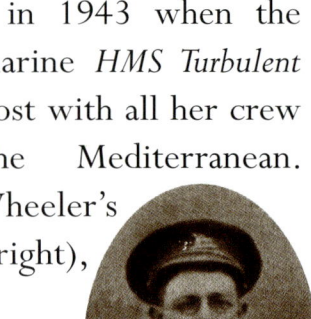

Back to the trenches

The biographies of the Sudbury men who died in the war reveal how common it was for wounded men to be sent back to the trenches several times after treatment, sometimes following serious injuries. Lance Corporal Charles Risby from a Cross Street family, went to France with the 2nd Suffolks in 1914, and was wounded three times in action including a serious stomach wound. Back in the trenches in 1917, he was taken a prisoner of war, dying in captivity two months later in Germany at the age of 25. His brother was a prisoner for most of the war having been captured in 1914 and was not freed until after the Armistice. He was probably taken prisoner when the 2nd Suffolks were overwhelmed at Le Cateau.

Former Stour bargeman Frederick Albon of the 7th Suffolks was wounded on the Somme in August 1916 and killed in action two months later. In 1918 his parents, mat weaver Frederick Albon and his wife Emma, lost their elder son Ernest fighting with the 2nd Suffolks in the Second Battle of the Somme.

Former shop worker Private Leonard Webb suffered from shell shock, a condition caused by the battle stress in which symptoms ranged in intensity, from an inability to function normally to physical and mental paralysis. It was so common that 29 specialist hospitals were needed in WWI to treat soldiers disabled by their symptoms. The former Sudbury shop assistant then died of wounds at a medical dressing station in October 1916, yet another casualty of the first Battle of the Somme. He was 23. His parents William Webb, the Sudbury manager for a large malting company, and his wife Edith lived at Stour Villas in Edgworth Road. Two years later their 20-year-old son Wallace was killed during the Advance to Victory just a month before the Armistice.

Taking over again

(going back to the trenches for the 20th time)

Back to the trenches tonight, boys!

Back to the trenches tonight.

We're going once more where the trench mortars roar,

Where bullets come 'futting' in many a score,

The 'sausage' and 'whizz bang,' we've heard them before;

And we've got to go on till the end of the War,

Unless we get touched for a Blighty, boys!

A Blighty one, cushy old Blighty.

Back to the trenches tonight, boys!

Back to the trenches tonight.

Yes, back to the water well up to the thigh,

And back to the rats and other small fry,

Our kits will be wet and our throats will be dry,

Where there's plenty to smell, but nothing to buy:

You can't buy a cushy old Blighty, boys!

A Blighty one, cushy old Blighty

Another of Army chaplain Stanley Mortimer Wheeler's war poems. Blighty was an slang word for home, a 'Blighty one' being a wound that did not maim, but serious enough to need treatment in the UK.

A forgotten airship raid

Through much of 1917 there were intermittent air raid warnings in Sudbury. Initially, air raid wardens were notified of a possible raider some way off then hooters sounded if there was imminent danger, this being known as the second call.

A diary kept by schoolboy George Austin Wheeler records twelve occasions in that year when he variously spotted airships or aircraft over the town or heard air raid warnings. He noted the last air raid warning of the year on the 19th of October, the night Sudbury was bombed for the second time by a Zeppelin. The incident seems to have been cloaked by the secrecy imposed in wartime. His diary corroborates a report sent to Suffolk Red Cross headquarters by a nurse at Belle Vue Red Cross Hospital describing how at the time of that air raid warning she heard bombs dropping nearby and spotted two fires. She found one and doused it with buckets of water.

These reports coincide with a large-scale German raid that very night when eleven Zeppelins set out to bomb industrial sites in the Midlands. It was a calm night but high altitude winds blew the airships south after they had crossed coastlines of Norfolk and Lincolnshire. A War Office map plots their erratic courses as they battled a 60-mile an hour gale at 20,000 feet. Four crossed Suffolk and at least two could have been responsible for dropping the incendiary bombs on Sudbury.

Six of the airships were subsequently blown over the Channel, four being either forced down or destroyed - one disappearing across the Mediterranean never to be seen again. The raiders dropped 273 bombs killing 36 people and injuring another 55, but this time Sudbury escaped with nothing worse than patches of scorched earth.

above : Official map of the Zeppelin raid
above right: George Wheeler, schoolboy diaryist
left : scan of his diary - the top entry noting the air raid warning

Torpedoed on a troopship

Troopships were prime targets for German U-boats and *SS Transylvania* had a full complement of 3,000 troops bound for Salonika in Greece when she was torpedoed off the Italian coast in May 1917. A second torpedo hit the crippled former liner as a Japanese destroyer was taking off survivors, and it sank almost immediately. More than 400 men were killed or drowned, their bodies coming ashore in France, Monaco and Spain but mostly on the Italian Riviera. Among them was that of John Coote, a 39-year-old soldier in the Northamptonshire Regiment, whose wife Priscilla was waiting for him at their home in Walnuttree Lane.

Private John Coote had done well for himself after a difficult start in life as one of a family of ten living in Ballingdon Street. At 13 he was working as a labourer but became a skilled carpenter and pattern maker. His employer had made a vain appeal against his conscription. Six months later, John Coot was one of 83 men from the *Transylvania* buried in the town cemetery at Savona, where a memorial commemorates another 275 who have no known grave. A comrade who survived by swimming eight miles to the shore wrote in a tribute: 'He was one of the best-liked men in the Company - he never complained and always carried on willingly.'

In June the previous year the destroyer *HMS Eden* sank in the English Channel after a collision with the *SS France*, a huge four-funnelled luxury French liner being used as a hospital ship. Surprisingly, it is difficult to find more about the collision apart from the fact that the liner survived to have a long life. Crew from the *Eden* are commemorated on a number of war memorials, among the dead was Able Seaman Henry John Belsham, of Sudbury, whose name is on the Chatham Naval Memorial to men lost at sea.

Torpedoed: SS Transylvania

Caught on camera - Harry Gould's last leave

above: Harry and wife Lydia right: Winifred and sister Marjorie in the portrait that went to war

Home on leave from France in 1917, Harry Gould took his wife and two small daughters to the modest studio of photographer Frank Dicks in North Street. He wanted to have a record what might be their last time together as a family. Prints of three photographs taken that day survive, one portraying seven-year-old Winifred Gould, in Alice band and patent shoes, holding her younger sister Marjorie's hand. Harry Gould took it back to France as a way of feeling close to his much-loved daughters and it was retrieved after his death and returned to his wife Lydia in Sudbury.

Few people owned cameras, so commercial photographers were kept busy taking portraits of husbands and sons in uniform. Among these was the studio of Emeny and Sons in Gainsborough Street which advertised as 'artistic photographers.'

A mite for the widow

The story of master butcher Harry Gould illustrates the huge scale of the Army's drain on manpower. He managed the London Central Meat Company's shop in Gainsborough Street, part of a large chain that sold cheaply through bulk buying which made it popular with the poor. In 1916 his employers applied for him to be exempted from military service because two thirds of their work force was already in uniform, forcing the closure of 85 of their shops. The tribunal granted a month's grace for Harry Gould but refused a second application.

In 1917 genial, affable Harry was slightly wounded fighting with the Cambridgeshire Regiment and then killed, aged 32, in the Third Battle of Ypres, shortly after being sent back to the trenches. His officer wrote to his widow Lydia, '… an enemy shell penetrated the shelter and so severely injured him that he died shortly afterwards. Before he expired he handed to me his watch which I am forwarding'.

But Harry's gold pocket watch was not in the bundle of his possessions that

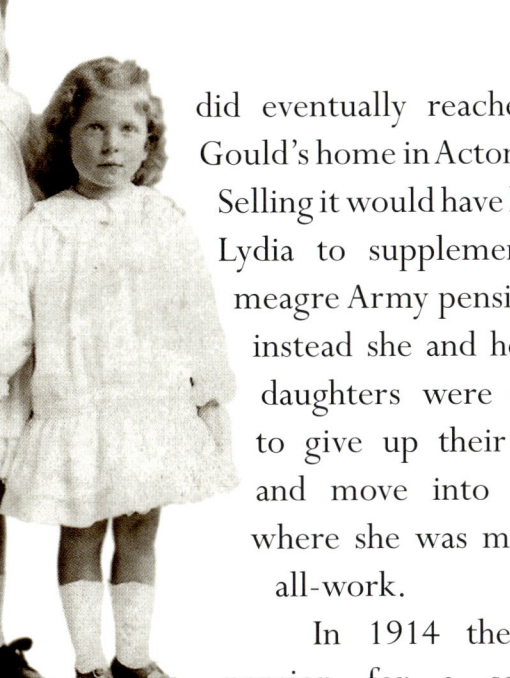

did eventually reached the Gould's home in Acton Lane. Selling it would have helped Lydia to supplement her meagre Army pension but instead she and her two daughters were forced to give up their home and move into a pub where she was maid-of-all-work.

In 1914 the basic pension for a soldier's widow was the equivalent of 70p a week granted for a year before it was reviewed. Cases were assessed and a typical grant in 1915 for a widow with two children was less than £1 a week.

In 1917 new applications reached 4-5,000 a week and a new Ministry of Pensions took over the task of dealing with payments. There were some increases, but the scale and temporary nature of the grants was barely adequate for the most basic subsistence. Lydia Gould eventually married a widower with children, this was the usual way for war widows to escape the poverty trap.

In the space of a few weeks in late 1917 Lydia lost her only brother as well as her husband. Sudbury carpenter and joiner Robert Hammond was killed fighting with the Leicestershire Regiment, he was 33 and married with children. His employers had won him three months respite from conscription so that he could complete an important contract before he went to war.

Far away from the war in the summer of 1917 a photographer caught this scene as a cavalry regiment rode down North Street

Lost in the mud of Passchendaele

1917

But for WWI, the small village of Passendale in West Flanders would have no significance in the wider world, but its old Dutch name of Passchendaele is remembered on three continents for huge loss of life and great suffering. It was the final objective in the Third Battle of Ypres, launched by the Allies on the last day of July 1917 in an attempt to break stalemate on this sector of the Western Front.

Record rainfall

It was almost a re-run of the Battle of Somme the year before, being fought in almost unimaginably harrowing conditions. The heaviest summer rainfall for decades turned reclaimed marshland into a swamp, and flooded trenches and the thousands of shell and bomb craters. Then the ground was further churned by ten days of Allied shelling intended to cut through barbed wire and weaken German defences, but these were so deep and well fortified that the bombardment largely failed.

Struggle in the morass

When whistles blew for the attack, the Allied infantry struggled through the mud to advance along a seven-mile front, impeded by the ammunition and extra equipment they carried, all the time being mown down by German machine-guns firing from pill boxes on higher ground. Men drowned in craters and flooded trenches and the bodies of the living and dead sank into the morass. The horrifying statistics reveal that the bodies of 90,000 British, Canadian, New Zealand and Australian troops were never identified and 42,000 more were not recovered. Such was the re-churning of the ground by shell fire that more than half the Sudbury men killed in the three main Ypres battles have no known grave.

Among the dead was Rifleman Herbert Basham, 29, who came from a family of silk weavers living in Plough Lane. His parents and three of his siblings earned their living at the loom. Private Arthur Claude Clark, 19, came from another family living in Plough Lane. His parents waited for more than a year before they were told that their 'missing' son was dead. His older brother Harry had died in Greece the previous year.

Battles claim father and son

Another battle casualty was Private John Cansdale, aged 30, who was married with children. His son Reginald was to die in WWII fighting with the 5th Suffolks on the day that Singapore fell in 1942. Mat weaver John Farrance and his wife Ellen living beside Ballingdon Bridge, had four sons in uniform. When the couple heard that their son Reginald had been lost in the battle they were still mourning his brother Alexander who had also been killed eleven months earlier on the Somme.

> Two Sudbury men were killed on one day in August. Lance Corporal Cyril Dale, 20, was the son of railwayman Arthur Dale and his wife Elizabeth living in Waldingfield Road, and Private Arthur Elmer came from a Cats Lane family of seven. The following day 19-year old Albert Newman became yet another fatality. His father Harry was an agricultural worker and his mother worked in the silk industry. The Newmans lived in Cross Street.

John and Emma Smith living in Station Road lost two of their sons. Harry, 37, died fighting at Passchendaele with the 2nd Suffolks. His older brother Ernest was killed in action eleven days before the Armistice. He was 43, married, and serving with a train division of the Army Service Corps. Before the war he had worked in the silk industry with his father. The battle ended early in November when the Canadians finally took the village of Passchendaele which by this time had been shelled into heaps of rubble. In 100 days of battle that gained five miles, Allied dead and wounded amounted to 500,000 - equivalent to half the present population of Birmingham. The following year the Germans regained virtually all the ground won at such great sacrifice, which is why Passchendaele became an international symbol of senseless military violence.

The line of the Western Front in 1917
(shows the extent of the German advance)

below : stretcher bearers struggling through deep mud at Passchendaele

photo courtesy Imperial War Museum IWM Q 005935

VC denied for a hero

Two thousand miles away from the Western Front, the British strategy of defending the Suez Canal and Persian oil had moved to offensive warfare with the aim of forcing the Turks out of Palestine and Israel. But in the Spring of 1917 the Allies twice failed to capture the town of Gaza which was important as the coastal gateway from Egypt.

In the second battle of Gaza the collection of medals earned by Sudbury men came close to including a Victoria Cross. Pioneer Horace Sore was recommended for a posthumous VC for what was described as 'a feat of exceptional gallantry' while serving as a signals specialist with the Royal Engineers. Despite heavy shelling he left cover on a mission to cut the Turks' telegraph link with their reinforcements. The 22-year-old signals specialist climbed a telegraph pole and had managed to cut one wire before he was blown to the ground by an exploding

Horace and Ernest Sore

shell. Undaunted, he climbed again and had succeeded in cutting a second wire before another shell blew him to pieces. 'He was absolutely devoid of fear,' an officer wrote to his mother Eliza at her home in East Street.

Horace Sore was recommended by his Brigadier for the Victoria Cross. But there were problems, neither his body nor his identity disc could be found and the NCO close to him had been killed soon after the incident. Horace's mother was told: 'It is hoped that the difficulty may be overcome and that the memory of Sudbury's gallant son will be justly honoured.' It was not to be - the name of Horace Sore was never added to the list of holders of the Victoria Cross nor was his sacrifice given any recognition. He is named on the Jerusalem Memorial.

Horace Sore came from a large family of seven sons and three daughters, all his brothers enlisting in the Army. His brother Ernest was killed fighting with the King's Dragoon Guards near Ypres in 1915. He had been a Scoutmaster in Sudbury, one of the first to be given the Royal Warrant. A cousin, Ezekiel Sore, died serving as a drummer with the Norfolk Regiment in what is now Iraq.

A letter of sympathy sent from the trenches to a Sudbury father, reveals the ordinary soldiers attitude to their Turkish adversaries at this time, and the very hard fighting in Gaza. The soldier, Private Beavis, wrote: 'It was a bit of a warm shout but we got through [the attack] all right and did well. I don't think there were many of us who did not make away with a few Johnny Turks. We were told that we had done all that was required except taking prisoners. Our reply was that the prisoners were there all right but that being 'a bit tired' they were having 'a long sleep.' So you can be proud that your son did his duty and made away with a few before he, poor lad, was himself called.'

1917

British, Australian and New Zealand forces, some mounted on camels, crossing the Sinai Desert before the push into Palestine

More action for 5th Suffolks

After the evacuation from Gallipoli, the 5th Suffolks joined the force defending the Suez Canal but were in front line action again in 1917. The Battalion fought in the second unsuccessful battle to take Gaza in which Sapper Horace Sore was killed, and the third in the Autumn of 1917 under the command of General Allenby. This was a decisive victory but cost more Sudbury lives. Before dawn the 5th Suffolks had gone over the top and through eight gaps in their barbed wire defences, facing machine gun and rifle fire as they attacked Turkish trenches in the sand dunes between Gaza and the sea. The British infantry advanced about two miles with the support of artillery and tanks, but there were heavy losses on both sides.

Three Sudbury men in the 5th Suffolks died that day. The first was Frank Harrison, son of groom and gardener George Harrison and his wife Ellen living in Cross Street. Their older son Ernest had died fighting in the Somme sector earlier in the year. Nineteen-year-old William Bunn was also a gardener's son, his family living in Ballingdon Street. The third death was that of 22-year-old Fred Keeble, who came through the action and was sleeping when he was killed 'practically instantaneously by a shell', a comrade wrote to his father widower Charles Keeble. All three are buried in the Gaza War Cemetery. Fred was the grandson of Harry Keeble, the 94-year-old who had slept through Sudbury's Zeppelin raid the previous year.

Commanding the 5th Suffolks was a hazardous business. Morriss Armes was killed in his first action at Gallipoli, his replacement Capt G Lacy Smith was invalided back to England seven weeks later, his temporary replacement Major Bowker served for only eight days, he was followed by Lt. Col. H J Miers who left owing to ill health less than four months later in February 1916. The Suffolks' Adjutant Major (later Lieut. Col.) Hervey Lawrence took over for six months until he handed over to Lt. Col. F H A Wollaston DSO. He commanded the Battalion at Gaza but was killed in an air raid in early 1918 while on leave in London.

Two more Sudbury men met their deaths fighting with the 15th Battalion, Suffolk Regiment, formed from the dismounted Suffolk Yeomanry. The battalion was part of three divisions which attacked the Turks' Gaza-Beersheba line near Sheria. Corporal George Mauldon, 25, was the son of brewer and hotel owner Christie Mauldon, who as mayor in 1902 had led the town's Coronation celebrations. Having older brothers in the brewing business, George had become a farmer at Ixworth and there are family memories of him being sent white feathers before he enlisted in the Suffolk Yeomanry. It was considered an elite cavalry regiment having a good sprinkling of Members of Parliament and Masters of Foxhounds in its ranks. Sergeant Fred Thompson was killed in the same action and was also buried in Beersheba War Cemetery in what is now Israel. He was only 19 and the son of Edward and Alice Thompson.

Sergeant George Mauldon on his mount

General Allenby enters Jerusalem on foot

The cost of this third battle for Ghaza in the harsh desert terrain was 18,000 British, Australian and New Zealand troops killed, wounded or missing. The following day the Turks pulled out of Gaza clearing the way for the capture of Jerusalem, the 5th Suffolks being in the guard of honour for General Allenby's triumphal entry into the city. For the first Christmas in centuries Jerusalem was in Christian hands. But there would be another major battle involving the 5th Suffolks and another year before the Regiment finally sailed from Beirut for Egypt in November 1918.

Christmas 1917 was understandably a muted affair in Sudbury with Mayor Alfred Howard attending a special service at Trinity Church in School Street to commemorate the men who had died and similar services were held at other churches in the town. Five names were added to the list that month among them that of Private Charles Crossley, a man in his early 40s who was well known in the town's silk industry having managed Fortune and Company and worked for Fennell's which later became Vanners. He was married and had children at school when he was killed in action in the Ypres Salient, as was Private Edward Blythe the 22-year-old son of Charles and Rosina Blythe.

The Allies built and maintained a vast network of railway lines in France for transporting troops, munitions and other supplies, as well as the wounded. Sapper William Cutmore served in the 277th Railways Company, Royal Engineers having been a platelayer with Great Eastern Railway. The son of mat maker Drewell Cutmore and his silk weaver wife Elizabeth living in Inkerman Row, he became yet another casualty in June 1917. He might have died of wounds as he was buried in Dozingham Military Cemetery in Belgium, one of three used by field hospitals and casualty stations in the area. The troops had difficulty with the Flemish names adapting them to 'Dozinghem, Bandaghem and Mendinghem.'

A long, painful road to victory 1918

The war becomes mobile

The New Year began the fifth at war without any obvious sign of an end to the struggle. There was stalemate in the trenches and food rationing on the home front. In Sudbury the dreaded telegrams telling of yet another death continued to arrive but not in any great number at first. Yet before the year was out the names of another 53 men would be added the list. At least 12 of them would be teenagers, mostly conscripted as soon as they reached 18 and speedily drafted overseas to man the trenches.

Russia was out of the war enabling Germany to switch 40 divisions from the East to the West Front and in March they launched a massive offensive on the Somme front, designed to snatch victory before the United States could fully deploy its troops. Before dawn on the first day they unleashed the greatest barrage of shells of the entire war - over a million in five hours. Then specially trained storm troopers infiltrated and by-passed the Allies front line strong points to cause disruption at the rear. The Germans outnumbered the British defenders by three to one and broke through the British Fifth Army inflicting 300,000 casualties (including 100,000 taken prisoner) and capturing 1,300 guns.

Warfare was mobile again, the Germans advancing 50 miles, the most achieved by either side since 1914, but then lost momentum through being unable to haul their guns over the devastation of the old Somme battlefield.

Twelve of the men on Sudbury War Memorial died in the first five weeks of the Spring Offensive, two dying of their wounds at the age of only 19. Private Charles White of the 11th Suffolks was the son of a retired police constable and his wife living in Clarence Road; Gunner Maurice Hempstead came from a family of brick workers employed at Chilton brickworks and living in Harp Close Road, Sudbury.

A week before the German attack the London Gazette Supplement announced the award of the Military Medal for bravery in the field to Private Percy Partridge of the 12th Suffolks. Citations were not printed, but the medal could only be awarded on the recommendation of a commander-in-chief in the field. Private Partridge's wife and children living in Weavers Lane must have been proud, but only a month later he was killed in action during the struggle to resist the German advance. He was 33. The award of a Military Medal to Sudbury-born Lance Corporal Ambrose Suttle was published in the same edition and he too became a dead hero that year. The agricultural worker enlisted in the 10th Battalion, Suffolk Regiment, but was killed in August fighting with the 24th Battalion, London Regiment in the Allied counter attack now known as the Second Battle of the Somme. The Suffolk Regiment deployed five battalions on the battlefields in this final year of the war.

A British soldier standing in a dump of shell cases left over from the second Battle of the Somme

1918

photo courtesy Imperial War Museum IWM Q 010943

Another bloodbath on the Somme battlefield

The greater part of Sudbury's losses in 1918 were in the counter attack launched in July, and in the final Advance to Victory which followed in late September as a series of battles in which British, French, Canadian and American armies, supported by tanks, forced the Germans back towards territory they had first occupied in 1914. In October the Allies broke through the Hindenburg line of defences, built by the Germans during the winter of 1916-17 and celebrated in the popular song of the day as the Siegfried Line, on which the British Tommies intended to 'hang out their washing.' The Germans were forced to abandon heavy equipment and supplies reducing their capacity to resist because their main supply line had been cut. In truth, both Armies were exhausted and the Armistice followed.

The conflict continued right up until the appointed time of 11am on the 11th day of the 11th month. There were some cheers in the trenches but most were just glad to turn their backs and walk away. Among the last Sudbury casualties to die was Private Walter Cook, 33, of the 13th Middlesex Regiment who died on the day before the Armistice. His parents lived in Princes Street.

No relief for a lucky survivor

Among the names on a war memorial on the main road from Arras to Cambrai is that of 22-year-old Private Robert Moore, one of almost 10,000 who died in the last three months of the war and who have no known grave. His story is a moving testament to both good fortune and the war machine's total disregard for the individual. At the outbreak of war he walked from his Ballingdon home to Bury St Edmunds to enlist, although he was only 17. He went to Gallipoli with the 5th Suffolks and twice survived a close encounter with death. In the first a bullet passed through his body to emerge just below his heart. Somehow he survived and was evacuated to a troopship, but that was torpedoed in the Mediterranean.

above: Robert Moore

Private Moore was barely alive when he was picked up six hours later and it took three years to nurse him back to health. Not for him a grateful nation and a pension, he was drafted to The Buffs (the East Kent Regiment) and sent to the Western Front two months before the end of the war, one of the many wounded pressed back into active service to fill gaps in the ranks.

He did not live to see Armistice - he was killed in September 1918 just six weeks before it was signed.

The 'boy' soldiers

There was a poignancy about the Sudbury losses in the last few months of the war because a disproportionate number of those killed were scarcely more than boys. Both British and German armies were so desperate for recruits that they sent conscripted youths to front line trenches with minimal training and without combat experience. The Army was not particular about checking ages either, and a reduction in the minimum height to only five feet (152 cm) enabled many headstrong teenagers to get into the war.

Private Archie Portfleet from a Gregory Street family, was only 17 when he was killed, having lied about his age in order to follow his four older brothers into uniform. His parents, mat maker Johannes and Clara Portfleet, had come to Sudbury when William Armes moved his matting business from Kings Lynn. Most of the Portfleet sons and a daughter followed their father into the factory. Herbert Debenham was a mat maker too and probably worked for the same firm. His 18-year-old son named after him, died in the same month as Archie Portfleet. The Debenhams were living in Suffolk Road after the war. Another 18-year-old fatality was Lance Corporal William Green who grew up in North Street as the son of stone and marble mason Edward Green and his wife Ada. More of Sudbury's young blood was spilt within three weeks of the Armistice being signed with the death of Private William Deaves, 18, of the Bedfordshire Regiment, son of a carpenter and from a family of nine living in Harp Close Road.

> Private John Parker left his home in this row of cottages to enlist under age without telling his mother. He went straight to the recruiting office instead of going to work as usual in a local factory. Angelina Parker never saw her son again, but had a letter from the trenches asking for 'brimstone and treacle' as he was suffering from worms. He was no more than 18 when he was killed in the Second Battle of the Somme in August 1918 and there is a family memory of his mother watching in dread as the telegram boy approached her door in Inkerman Row. These mid-19th century weavers' cottages were demolished in the 1970s to make way for Playford Court. The large windows on the first floor shed maximum light on looms but the lavatory was in the garden together with a tin bath. This was brought into the house for the weekly bath night, the water shared by the whole family.

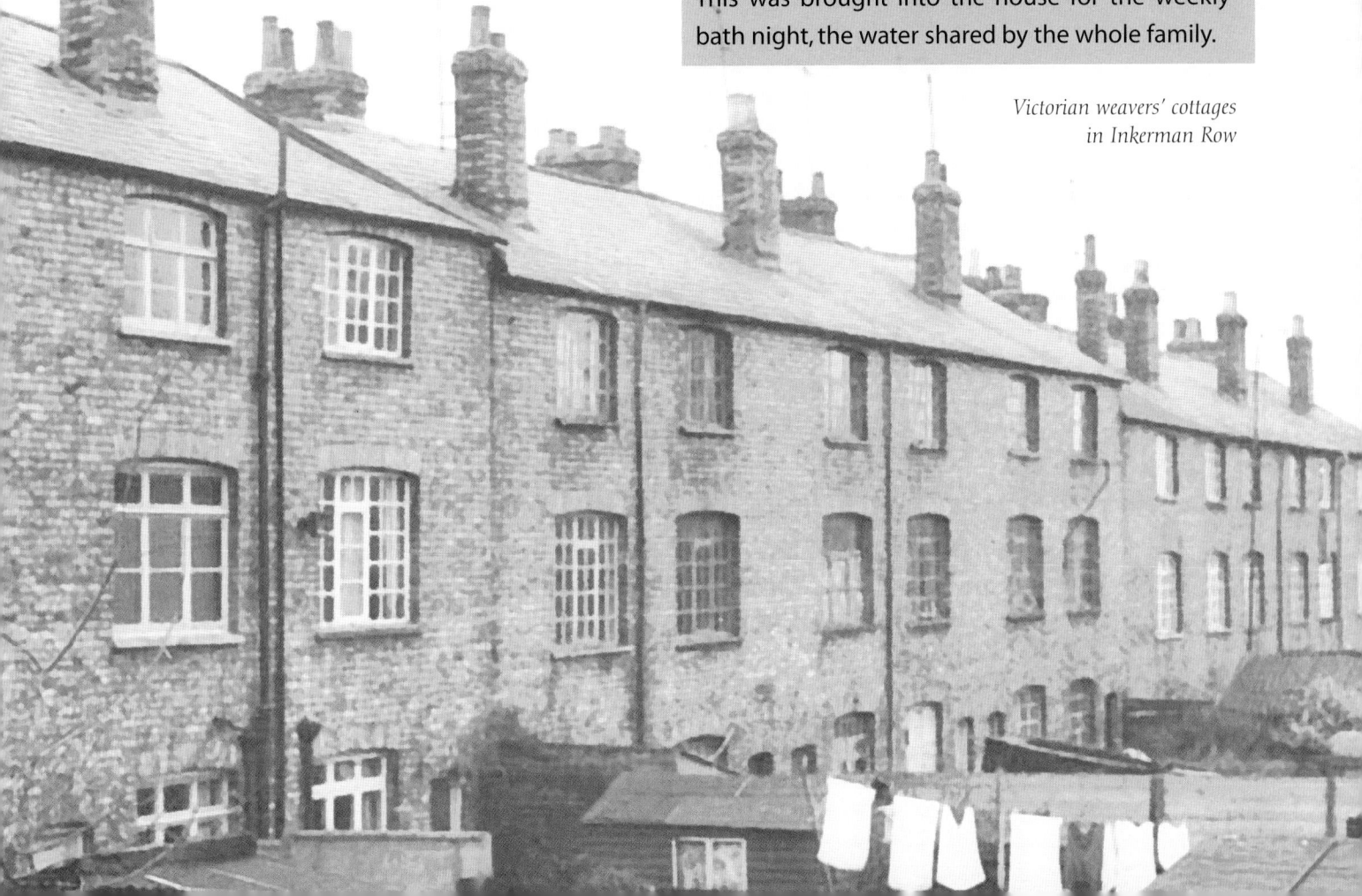

Victorian weavers' cottages in Inkerman Row

Gas - the silent killer in the trenches

The use of poison gas as a weapon is one of the horrors often associated with the First World War and was used extensively during 1918. The German Army was the first to use it on the Western Front with an attack in April 1915. In the following month, men of the 2nd Suffolks were among its victims, the chlorine gas causing vomiting, difficulty in breathing and a burning sensation in the eyes, nose and lungs. The British later retaliated in kind, both sides using gas weapons for much of the war despite having signed the Hague Convention of 1899 that banned their use.

The initial intention was to put enemy troops out of action rather than to kill, but by the end of the war more than 88,000 of all nationalities had died from the effects of gas weapons. More than 8,000 of these casualties died serving in British and Empire forces. Another 185,000 of them needed treatment. Chlorine and phosgene gasses were followed in 1917 by mustard gas which became the most feared, as it arrived in shell fire as a seemingly innocuous liquid that gradually evaporated. It was usually hours before victims began vomiting and choking, with tell-tale yellow blisters forming on any exposed skin. Mustard gas burned the body both externally and internally, and men effectively drowned as their damaged lungs filled with yellow fluid. Victims with serious external burns could be in agony for weeks before they died, sometimes having to be strapped down to keep them in their beds.

It is difficult to ascertain how many of the men named on Sudbury War Memorial died from the results of gas weapons. Relatives were frequently told that men had died of wounds rather than specifying gas, and the records of many who served in WWI were destroyed by enemy action in WWII. Certainly mustard gas is blamed for causing one in every seven casualties in the Third Battle of Ypres in 1917 in which at least 20 Sudbury men died.

The fear of gas poisoning lived on for decades after the war. The perceived threat of gas being used as a weapon in WWII led to extensive anti-gas measures being taken by all the combatants.

The worst legacy of all the gasses was lung damage and with it a greater risk of later developing tuberculosis and cancer. Long after the Second World War, Sudbury GP Dr Alan McLauchlan, was still treating old soldiers suffering from the effects of being exposed to gas in WWI.

> Suffolk Regiment soldier Walter Gibbons was treated at Belle Vue Red Cross Hospital for the after effects of being gassed in WWI. As part of his therapy he stitched the Suffolk Regiment badge in the frame over his bed. Despite long-term treatment he only partially recovered, dying in 1930 at the age of 48. He lived in Sudbury with his family and wife Ethel, a tiny woman less than five feet tall, who struggled in poverty for years to raise their seven children on a small pension she supplemented by making and selling children's clothes.

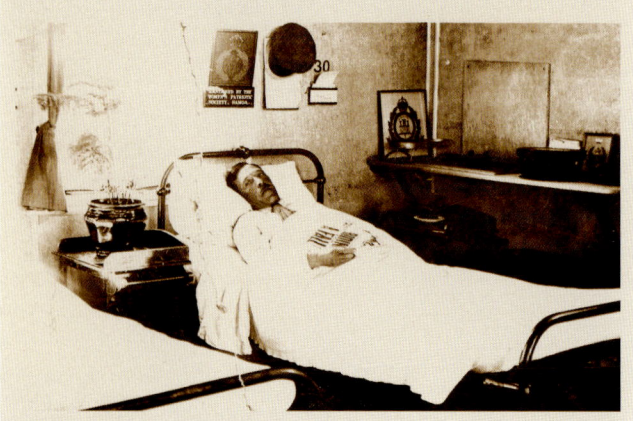

Walter Gibbons at Belle Vue Hospital

The victim of gassing

The story of Private Oliver Ratcliffe of the 2nd Suffolks is an example of the suffering caused by gas weapons. He was gassed twice according to a local newspaper report, and died at the age of 34 after suffering a mental breakdown.

His widowed mother Florence Ratcliffe, living in Meadow Lane, learned that he had been treated in hospital for the effects of gassing and then returned to front line duty, only to be disabled again by this much-feared weapon. This second occasion was possibly at the Battle Loos in September 1915 when the British used gas against German troops for the first time, only for it to blow back into their own lines where it is said to have caused more casualties than in the enemy trenches. The gas used on this occasion was chlorine.

Oliver Ratcliffe was treated in hospital in the UK and then sent to the Battalion's Depot at Bury St Edmunds. He was a regular soldier who had fought in the Boer War and must have experienced most of the traumas of soldiering, but the horror of being gassed seems to have had a serious psychological affect on him, perhaps causing extreme terror at the thought of being sent back to the trenches. The newspaper report of his death continues: 'After going to Colchester where he visited friends, he showed signs of mental trouble after his terrible experience and was admitted to a Colchester [Military] Hospital where he died.' He was buried at Colchester with full military honours in March, 1916, being described as 'a fine soldier with an excellent regimental record.'

The British Army was initially ill-prepared for gas attacks, the only protection being a wet pad held across the nose and mouth, some men swearing that a cloth soaked in urine worked best. Gas masks had been issued by the time the British used chlorine gas at the Battle of Loos but when it blew back towards their own trenches, men tore off their masks because of difficulty in breathing and because condensation clouded their vision.

Later designs were more efficient, though not effective against the insidious and much-feared mustard gas unless it was spotted before men came into contact with it. Gas alerts were well organised, with warnings being sounded by honking horns and beating on empty shell cases positioned along the trenches.

British troops blinded by tear gas awaiting treatment at Flanders in 1918

Four times unlucky

The death in July 1918 of Lance Corporal Thomas Edward Currie is another tragic example of the way the wounded were treated in order to feed the war effort. He was sent back to the Front three times after being wounded and was then killed during the Allied counter attack. He was still only 19. His cousin Edward 'Ted' Hills, had been killed in action the previous year at the same age. They were both members of the Hills family of watchmakers and jewellers, both answering to the name Ted, which must have caused some confusion.

Thomas 'Ted' Currie had left his job with a confectioner on Market Hill after persuading a recruiting sergeant that he was old enough to fight. He enlisted in the Seaforth Highlanders as a tribute to his Scots-born father who had died when he was baby. After his three brushes with death on the battlefield he was convinced his luck must run out and gave away his watch on his last home leave. The writer of the customary letter sent from the battlefield after his death apologised to his widowed mother for lack of information, 'as all the officers in his company were casualties.' His burial place is unknown but his name is on a memorial commemorating men who died on the Marne in July 1918.

His cousin Edward Hills also enlisted under age. He was only 17 when he left his apprenticeship as a watchmaker in the family business to enlist in the Suffolk Regiment.

Lance Corporal Ted Currie

Ted Hills had been a keen athlete and sportsman at Sudbury Grammar School and expected to eventually take over the family firm. He was a 19-year-old sergeant instructor when he was killed in April 1917 during the Battle of Arras, a five-week offensive to take German lines on high ground. It failed to achieve a major breakthrough and stalemate followed. He is one of almost 35,000 on the Arras memorial to men who have no known grave.

Sergeant Instructor Ted Hills

Five Sudbury men died in Greece as the Allies fought the Bulgarians who had sided with the Axis powers. Sergeant Charles Spalding, originally of the 5th Suffolks, was serving with the 1st Battalion, Northamptonshire Regiment which suffered heavy casualties at Doiran in Greece. Bulgaria surrendered in late September and he died in early November aged 35. He was married to Frances who was living at Batt Hall on the Bulmer Road after the war.

A hot mustard tip

Prisoner of war Private Martin of Ballingdon thought of a way to make the bread he was given more palatable - it was probably made of rye. He asked his mother to send him mustard to spread on it. His widowed mother had three other sons in the army, among them could have been 24-year-old Private Basil Martin of Ballingdon Street who died of wounds in France in 1917.

Success at a high price

In September 1918 the 5th Suffolks fought, in what was then Palestine, at the decisive battle of Megiddo which led to the destruction of the Ottoman armies. The main attack began early on the 19th with a combined attack from sea, air and on land. By the end of the day the Turks were in disorderly retreat, but not without cost. Among the dead were two more of Sudbury's bright young men.

Private Stanley Nunn, 24, had survived Gallipoli and the battles for Gaza only to die on that day. He had kept in close touch by letter with his parents, his father James Nunn was a departmental manager in one of Sudbury's silk weaving companies. He and his wife commemorated their son in an unusual way by changing the name of their house in Cornard Road to Stanley Villa.

At the age of 23, Lance Corporal John Jay of the Fifth Suffolks' was another seasoned campaigner. He had a remarkable escape at Gallipoli when a shell burst smashed his rifle but left him unharmed. But in September one of the dreaded telegrams from the War Office informed his parents living in Meadow Lane, that he had been killed in Palestine. His father Arthur Jay was in business as a plumber and decorator.

Disease took a heavy toll among the troops serving in the Middle East. Among them was Sergeant Bertie Lorking of the Machine Gun Corps who died of pneumonia in hospital in Alexandria in October. His parents, plasterer William Lorking and his wife Emma, lived in Newmans Road. In Sudbury's original Roll of Honour he was recorded as having been 'recommended for a decoration.'

In the same month Sergeant Harry Daniels of the Army Service Corps died of a fever in Egypt. His parents, gardener Harry Daniels and his wife Achsah, living in Garden Row, had already lost their older son Frederick killed fighting in France with the Essex Regiment. He was a father of two.

above: Private Stanley Nunn killed at Megiddo, wearing both the standard khaki uniform and khaki drill issued for hot climates

below: A cheerful mounted officer leads a column of Turkish prisoners after the Battle of Megiddo

photo courtesy Imperial War Museum IWM Q 012326

Influenza - the new enemy

In the spring of 1918 a new enemy had entered the arena: a virulent form of influenza that swept much of the world in the following two years killing at least 20 million people. It was erroneously called Spanish flu though it had been first identified in the United States.

The pandemic spread quickly, killing thousands of soldiers who had survived the bullet and the shell, many as they waited in northern France for repatriation and others after they returned home. Children and the elderly are usually most at risk during flu epidemics but many victims of this virus were young adults, one explanation being that older generations had better resistance through having survived an epidemic 20 years earlier.

Most of those who became sick with flu in the Spring of 1918 survived, but the virus mutated to a far more deadly strain that could kill within days. Initial symptoms were those of a fairly severe bout of flu (fever, headache, sore throat and cough), but this often become pneumonia resulting in a blue tinge to the lips indicating that the victim's lungs were filling with blood or mucus. Death usually followed in 24 to 48 hours.

It's not known how many people died in this way in Sudbury, but in the peak year of 1919 there were 154 burials in the town cemetery, almost double the total of 1917. In February 1919 North Street school was closed because of the pandemic together with another on the Croft. That month there were 24 deaths in the town from the pneumonic form of flu and more than 40 altogether, 14 of the victims being inmates of the Workhouse.

> Amongst all the Commonwealth Graves Commission headstones in Sudbury cemetery is that commemorating 19-year-old Private James Parish of the 5th Suffolks, who died in a London Hospital on Christmas Day 1917 from severe wounds inflicted in Palestine. Beside it, is the grave of his father and a sister who died in the space of four days in February 1919, which was at the height of the flu pandemic in Sudbury. James Parish senior, made and sold confectionery in Gainsborough Street, living over the shop with his family including 15-year-old Madeline who died four days later.

The soldier victims

Some of the men on the Sudbury War Memorial who died in the pandemic can be positively identified. Master butcher Joseph Blythe and his wife Sarah living in Church Street heard that their son Maurice had died of it in France ten days before the Armistice. He was 30 and a corporal in the Royal Engineers. Twenty-one-year-old Frederick Adams was another definite victim. His parents lived in Melford Road, his father earning his living as a mat maker and his mother as a horsehair weaver. Their son had fought in the Balkans and the war had been over for more than a month when he died there of the deadly virus.

William and Sarah Stearns of East Street would never have forgotten the date their son died from flu, Driver John Stearns, serving in France with the Royal Engineers, became a victim on Armistice Day - 11th November. Charles Barrell from a Bulmer family returned from fighting all through the war with the Grenadier Guards only to die of the virus in March 1919. He was 32, over six feet (183cm) tall and had survived being severely wounded in 1915. His wife Florence, living in Mill Lane with their son Charlie, was told he had been taken ill after a parade for the King, dying in a London hospital. In the same month fatalities in the Sudbury area including 22-year-old Winifred Sillitoe whose parents owned the Ship and Star pub in Friars Street, and Eva Raymond, the 34-year-old daughter of the Rector of Middleton.

After this peak early in 1919 the number of cases in Sudbury began to decline but globally the pandemic lasted until the summer of 1920. It had killed an estimated 30,000 British troops and 225,000 civilians.

Colonel Percy Elliston Allen, of Ballingdon Hall, came home after service with the Royal Army Service Corps, only to die from the flu in 1919. He was 53, and owner of the Allen brickworks.

Death in a prison camp

A possible victim of the pandemic was Private Ernest Lever, one of the six children of publican Harry Lever of the Plough pub in Melford Road and his wife Agnes. The young soldier had returned to France in March 1918 after home leave having been a witness at the marriage of his sister Lily. She waved him off from the house as he disappeared down North Street, never to see him again. He was captured shortly after returning to the Front and died, aged 20, in a German prisoner-of-war camp at Kassel, only a week before the Armistice. Scouting in Sudbury lost one of its mainstays with his death as he was a founder member of the 3rd Sudbury Scout Troop. His nephew Ernest Shaw was named after him, and devoted his long life to the Scout movement playing a major role in the fund-raising efforts that resulted in a purpose-built headquarters for the 3rd Sudbury Troop in Quay Lane.

Returning prisoners of war spoke bitterly of their treatment at the hands of their German captors after they began to emerge from behind the peace line about a week after the Armistice, many badly malnourished and in rags. Some former prisoners of war failed to recover from the deprivation. Sidney Leeks of the 2nd Suffolks died in St Leonard's Hospital three years later. He had been taken prisoner in 1914 when the Regiment was overwhelmed at Le Cateau and spent the duration of the war in prison camps in both Germany and Russia. He was described as 'broken in health' when he was finally demobbed. He was 34 when he died and was living at Great Waldingfield.

Long-term malnutrition caused a significant number of deaths. At Christmas 1918, one former prisoner said that his main meal on Christmas Day the previous year had consisted of cabbage and mangold, a root vegetable used for animal feed.

above left : Colonel Percy Elliston Allen
above right: Private Ernest Lever

Anguish, anger and commemoration

Anger in the ranks

The war was over at last, but January 1919 began badly in Sudbury with broken men beginning to return from the battlefields to find that they had little prospect of a job, and that the town was in the throes of the influenza pandemic and food rationing.

Many of homecomings were still many months away because the Army was struggling with the logistics of demobbing more than 3 million men, preference was being given to the youngest and to those who could prove they had a job waiting. It led to resentment and frustration among those kicking their heels in France and in transit camps in the UK. In January 10,000 troops camped on the South Coast marched into Folkestone. The promise of a week's leave appeased them but when the military reneged on it they marched back into town, this time armed with their rifles. The leave demanded by the troops was at last granted.

In Sudbury, the Town Council debated ways of commemorating the war and decided to apply for a suitable trophy from the battlefields to put on permanent show. They had in mind a large German artillery gun or a trench mortar. The idea was soon dropped for lack of interest, in truth everyone was heartily sick of the war and everything to do with it. Even compiling a Roll of Honour of those who had served in the war proved to be more difficult than expected. People were either slow in returning forms seeking information, or else ignored them altogether. The Council decided that no reasonable expense should be spared to achieve a complete list, and canvassers went from door to door. In July 1919 the line was drawn at 1,400 officers and men, of whom 218 had died. Time has proved that the list of dead was even longer than the total arrived at in the summer of 1919.

How Sudbury Town Council's idea for a permanent memorial on Market Hill might have looked

The figure now accepted is 241 including the five killed in the Zeppelin raid of 1916.

The Council agreed that all those who went to war would be treated equally on the Roll of Honour and it should be inscribed, illuminated and hung in the Town Hall. At some point the Council's decision was countermanded, and the end result is a rather insignificant leather bound book - the white leather now rather grubby - with the names listed in black ink on lined paper in a fashion that resembles a business ledger.

Farewell to an old warrior

Another name was added to the list of dead in January. Company Sergeant Major John French was a man with a charmed life, or so it seemed. The 48-year-old veteran had fought through the Gallipoli campaign with the 5th Suffolks, being both an inspiration and a father figure. He must have had plenty of brushes with death as the battalion struggled to survive against the Turks' ferocious defence, disease and the elements. He had written home of one near miss when a shell blew him over, but he escaped unscathed.

He fought with the 5th Suffolks for possession of Gaza and was with them though the long campaign to push the Turks out of Palestine where they sustained losses, but John French came through. Along the way, he was three times mentioned in despatches and awarded the Distinguished Conduct Medal (DCM). The citation published in the London Gazette reads: 'For conspicuous gallantry and devotion to duty over an extended period of operations and especially during two engagements when he set a splendid example to his men by his coolness under fire and the ability with which he performed his duties.'

John French was expected to return to manage the family-owned printing and stationery business in King Street, but just two months into the peace, he lost his life to a bout of dysentery. The Acting Regimental Sergeant Major died in Cairo as he and his men were waiting to be demobbed.

Post-war casualties at sea

The war was over on the Western Front but British forces were still in action. In August 1919 a British-led expeditionary force took the north Russian port of Archangel without opposition, in order to support the White Russians in their struggle against the Bolsheviks. The British warship *HMS Vittoria* was torpedoed and sunk by Bolshevik submarine *Pantera* in the Baltic. All but eight of her crew were saved by another destroyer, but among those who died was Able Seaman John Pettitt, the 18-year-old son of assistant surveyor Horace Pettitt and his wife Emily who lived in Priory Road.

A month later the eldest son of Revd. John Milner, chaplain to Sudbury Workhouse and Rector of Chilton, became another casualty of the campaign. Revd. Dermod Ross Milner broke his neck falling from a ship's ladder while serving as a chaplain on the hospital ship *Garth Castle*. He died, aged 29, and was buried at Archangel.

Workhouse chaplain John Milner and his family out for a spin in his 1905 French Gladiator

'Pennies' for the Dead

Early in 1919 brown cardboard packages containing bronze memorial plaques began to arrive at homes all over the country. The one (shown right) sent to miller James Hagger and his wife Ellen in Upper East Street, commemorates their 20-year-old son Frank who enlisted underage and died in France in 1917. The Government dispatched more than a million to next of kin as a token of the nation's gratitude, together with a memorial scroll. In this instance the name cast on James Hagger's plaque was misspelt.

The design was chosen from more than 800 entered in a Government-sponsored competition and the £250 first prize went to Liverpool sculptor Edward Carter Preston. It depicts Britannia in classical robes and helmet holding a laurel wreath with a symbolic lion at her side. The dolphins in the background refer to Britain's sea power, and the tribute 'He died for freedom and honour' around the edge, had been stipulated in the rules. There was controversy over the section below Britannia's feet depicting an eagle, symbolic of the enemy, being subjugated by a lion. Critics suggested it might prove unhelpful in post war relations with the former enemies of Britain and her Allies.

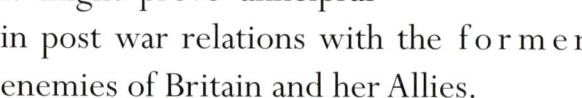

The plaques were cast from 150 tonnes of bronze at a cost of about four shillings (20p) each, supposedly financed from German reparation money. Unfortunately, production and delivery were not a complete success and the scheme ended before all next of kin had received this official recognition due to them. Not all the recipients were pleased with the plaques, which were often disparagingly referred to as Death Pennies or a Dead Man's Penny, regarding them as a poor return for a life needlessly lost.

above left: James Hagger   above: His plaque
below left: Advert for Hills' plaque holder

TO ALL WHO HAVE LOST IN THE WAR.

WAR MEMORIAL PLAQUE
OR PHOTO HOLDER.

7/6 & 10/- each.
SOLE AGENT FOR SUDBURY—
EDWARD HILLS
FRIARS ST., SUDBURY.

A plaque sent to the family of a 5th Suffolk soldier who fought at Gallipoli was found long after the war in the Stour near Ballingdon Bridge. It was in memory of Private Percy Hume who died on the island of Malta where casualties from Gallipoli were treated. He was the son of lime burner John Hume and his wife who raised their family in Ballingdon Street, and it emerged that the plaque had been tossed into the river by 21-year-old Percy's brother. He might well have considered it too slight a recognition of a much-loved sibling. The plaque, and a medal found with it, were subsequently returned to the family.

1919

In Flanders Fields the poppies blow
Between the crosses row on row,
That mark our place; and in the sky
The larks, still bravely singing, fly
Scarce heard amid the guns below

From a poem written by Canadian Army surgeon Lieutenant Colonel John McCrae (1872-1918), as he watched poppies blowing in the wind beside the grave of a young soldier he had buried the previous night.

The survivors organise

There was much anger and bitterness in post-war Sudbury. The town that the returning soldiers and sailors had left to go to war had moved on, and those who had left it as boys came home as men. They wanted work and they needed rehabilitation and, not surprisingly, believed they were owed something after their sacrifice, particularly the conscripts who had been forced to fight.

Certificate of 'Comrades' membership

A Sudbury branch of the Comrades of the Great War was founded in March with the object of helping them, but the survivors were determined to help themselves. They flocked to join a new branch of the National Association of Discharged Sailors and Soldiers which initially met at the White Horse. Nationally the organisation formed strong links with the trade unions and in May members massed at a rally in Hyde Park before marching on Parliament, on the way throwing missiles at women bus conductors who they blamed for taking men's jobs. The Bolshevik revolution had cast a long shadow and the Government was understandably worried, particularly since riots in Germany were being attributed to Communist influences. In response the British Establishment - with the help of the Press barons - put its weight behind the Comrades of the Great War, and in 1921 this amalgamated with other ex-servicemen's organisations to form the British Legion that now has a Royal prefix.

Two months after the launch of the British Legion Sudbury formed its own branch which has remained strong and active through all the years since. Nationally and locally the Legion has campaigned for the veterans and given them practical support which now extends to ex-servicemen and women from many conflicts including those of the twenty first century.

The Legion's symbol of Remembrance is the poppy, chosen because it bloomed defiantly on the devastated battlefields in northern France where so many hundreds of thousands had died. In 1922 a new factory was set up by the Disabled Society to make artificial poppies in aid of ex-servicemen and women and their dependants. The original poppy was designed to be easily assembled by workers with a disability, and that principle remains. More than 70 per cent of the employees have a disability or suffer from a chronic illness. Millions of Britons buy the poppies in November by way of a donation to the Royal British Legion, both as a symbol of Remembrance for the dead and to support veterans and their families needing help.

Celebrating the peace

The guns were put aside on Armistice Day, but the war was not officially over until the signing of the Peace Treaty at Versailles in June 1919. Germany was required to disarm, accept blame for starting the war, cede territory, and make crippling reparations. The harsh terms imposed by the Allies

A horse-drawn float enters North Street on Peace Day

caused anger and resentment that festered in Germany and came to be blamed for the aggression which led to WWII.

The 19th of July was designated Peace Day and Sudbury put on its brightest face for a day-long celebration the like of which had never been seen before. The Town Council hung out flags and urged the population to decorate homes and shops. Church bells rang and the man from the Suffolk Free Press reported that the crowd thronging Market Hill was larger than those seen at the celebrations for either Queen Victoria's Diamond Jubilee or the Coronations of her son and grandson.

A carnival procession with two bands formed up on the Croft before winding its way around the town led by the Mayor and town dignitaries. The children were not left out, 1,200 of them cheering and waving flags before going to Belle Vue meadow for more celebrations. Guides and Scouts marched, and the khaki worn by Sudbury Grammar School Army Cadet Corps brought cheers from the spectators, who wore their Sunday best for the occasion.

More than one float in the procession carried the banner 'To the Boys who fought and died,' but there was a notable lack of any organised participation by ex-soldiers. This was probably because the East Anglian federation of ex-servicemen organisations had ordered a boycott of Peace Day celebrations out of anger that money was being spent in this way when their need of jobs and homes was so pressing.

The procession finally came to a halt at the cricket ground in Friars Street where the judges awarded prizes to floats and equestrians. Patients at the Belle Vue Red Cross Hospital were treated to a celebration dinner, and the day ended with dancing on the Market Hill, a fancy dress dance at the Drill Hall, and finally fireworks. It was a day to remember in the harsh years of the Depression that were ahead.

The Story of Sudbury War Memorial

In early 1919 Sudbury had begun to consider what might constitute a fitting memorial to its lost husbands and sons, two in every five of them having no known grave. Suggestions were discussed at a public meeting at the Town Hall in April. On the short list were a recreation ground, a children's ward for St Leonard's Hospital and a 'social institute.' But Mayor Alfred Howard was strongly opposed to any memorial being a charge on the rates, and the unanimous decision was to raise 'an ancient British cross of heroic size' financed by public subscription. 'It should symbolise blood, agony and bitterness of soul,' urged mill owner Isaac Clover, who had lost his eldest son and two brothers-on-law in the war. However, the meeting decided by a small margin, to research the possibilities of providing a recreation ground in York Road, but nothing came of this.

The design chosen for the memorial was the Cross of Sacrifice now seen in Commonwealth War Graves Commission cemeteries around the world. Eminent Edwardian architect Sir Reginald Blomfield designed the Latin cross in limestone with a bronze sword pointing downwards on the face. The Cross represents the faith of most of the dead and the sword is the warrior's weapon at rest. Sudbury's Cross was produced from the original design by monumental sculptor Frederick Linley of North Street.

There were long arguments about where it should be erected, suggestions included the Old Market Place, Market Hill and the town cemetery. The Town Council suggested St Peter's churchyard, an idea promptly dismissed by the War Memorial Committee on the grounds that it was not publicly-owned land. The eventual choice of location was on an island in the roadway close to the Freemasons' Hall in North Street, but it has since been moved twice for traffic reasons. The final re-location to outside St Gregory's churchyard followed the closure of North Street to through traffic.

The unveiling

A huge crowd gathered for the unveiling and dedication on the first Sunday in October 1921, most of the women dressed in black. The Suffolk Free Press reported people standing in roads converging on the site and watching from every vantage point as a military band played. The Territorials of the 5th Suffolk Regiment, who had lost so many comrades, were there led by Lieut. Col. Brian Oliver. Captain Dean led the expanding British Legion and Sudbury Grammar School Army Cadet Corps were smart in their uniforms. Local Boy Scouts were joined by others from Glemsford, Long Melford and Henny and the Sudbury Girls School sent its League of Honour supervised by headmistress Miss Poole.

Superintendent Reeve and Inspector Cole of the borough police led the procession of the Mayor and Corporation in their robes, followed by the diocesan Bishop, local clergy and a united church choir. Sudbury Fire Brigade was on parade too, and Commandant Mrs Margaret Rix and Sister Vera Chater represented Belle Vue Red Cross Hospital.

The occasion would have merited inviting a much be-ribboned General or

top: Scene at the dedication of the memorial

above: Flowers on the upper shelf were removed to prevent staining the pristine limestone

above: After WWII the memorial was moved westwards to improve traffic flow

below: The Memorial on the move again to its present site outside St Gregory's churchyard

the Lord Lieutenant of Suffolk to unveil the memorial, but Sudbury had special reasons for its choice. The honour went to Lieut. Colonel Hervey Lawrence DSO, the 5th Suffolks' former adjutant who had shared the men's deprivation and dangers at Gallipoli. 'He was beloved by all the Regiment and they looked up to him as a father or elder brother,' the Mayor told the gathering. 'If the warriors named on this memorial had a say as to who they would like to unveil it, the name of Colonel Lawrence would at once have been suggested. He lost so many men whose names are on this memorial that he must have great sympathy with the relatives, more sympathy than a stranger whether he be a Lord Lieutenant, General or even a Field Marshal.'

A fitting tribute

The Colonel was obviously moved: 'I feel that the spirits of these men are with us today,' he said, and went on to describe the memorial as a fitting tribute to bear witness to the present and future generations of the honour and love borne for those who had fallen for King and Country.

Sudbury expressed its emotion in flowers. They were piled high around the memorial, covering the base and the plinth right up to the foot of the Cross, so many that it was feared that they might discolour the white limestone. Early the next day those on the top ledge were quietly removed. Originally the names of the war dead were inscribed on the stone base but some had become illegible by the end of WWII, and the names of the fallen from both World Wars are now listed on bronze panels.

A focus for mourning

The memorial has provided a focus for both civic and personal mourning in the years that followed, graves and memorials overseas being inaccessible to ordinary families for many decades because of the cost of travelling abroad. Flowers, some ornate wreaths others gathered from gardens and fields, would regularly appear at its base to mark anniversaries in the life or death of the warriors named on the bronze panels.

The Bishop's advice

They have not been forgotten, nor should they be, but the Bishop of St Edmundsbury's exhortation on that October day in 1921 took a much wider view. He told the gathering: 'There was much in the war that we all want to forget. We shall do well not to remember the bitterness, the hatreds, the righteous anger that made us struggle to the end against our enemy.'

A generation later another 60 names of Sudbury's war dead would be added to the 241 already on the memorial.

Sir Reginald Blomfield was in his 60s when he designed the Cross of Sacrifice. He is also the architect of the huge Menin Gate Memorial at Ypres to British and Commonwealth troops who died in the Ypres salient and have no known grave. His public works include Lambeth Bridge and re-modelling part of Regent Street and the north side of Piccadilly Circus. He died in 1942 and the memorials he designed to commemorate millions are his memorial too.

A civic welcome home

In September 1919 the people of Sudbury organised a Welcome Home supper for the veterans back from the war. They feasted on roast mutton, beef and pork, chicken and ham, followed by apple, jam and plum tarts as well as jelly, custard and cheese. There were so many veterans that the party at the Drill Hall in Gainsborough Street, was divided between the main hall and the annexe. Mayor Hammond Alston proposed the toasts in the hall, and the Town Clerk in the annexe. The most solemn moment, no doubt coloured by vivid memories, was when hosts and their guests raised glasses to toast 'Our Fallen Brothers.' But entertainment by the Verilites concert party lifted the mood, the whole gathering joining in popular music hall songs of the day.

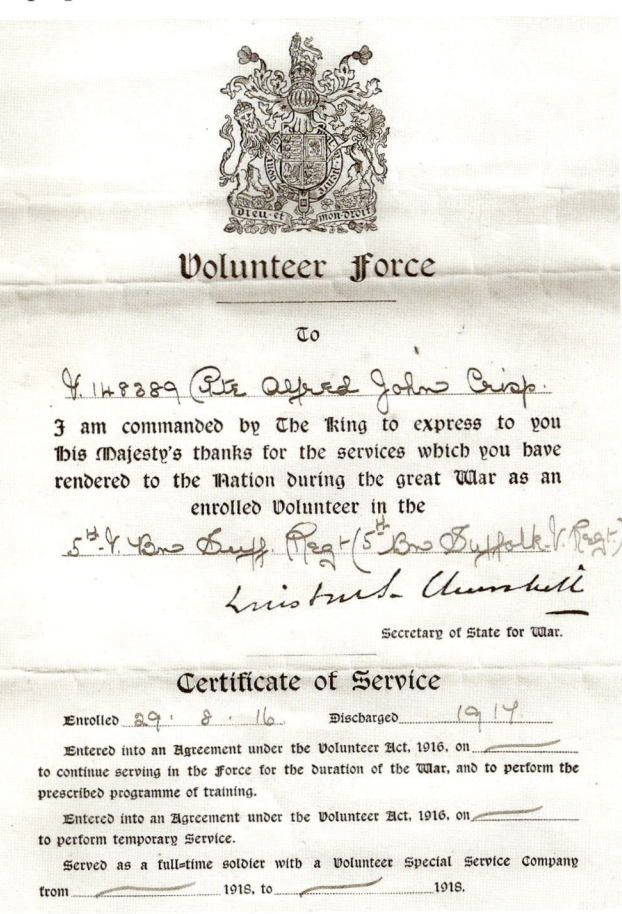

Royal thanks for a Sudbury volunteer

Lieut. Colonel Hervey Lawrence, who unveiled the War Memorial, came from a family with a long military tradition and was a descendant of Sir Henry Lawrence, killed at the siege of Lucknow during the Indian Mutiny. The Colonel had also served in India, as well as during the Boer War, and at the age of 28 was appointed Adjutant of the 5th Suffolks while serving with the Cameronians (The Scottish Rifles) at Colchester. At that time he was playing cricket for his native county of Kent. In 1918 he commanded the 1st Herefordshire Regiment in France and was both wounded and decorated, including the Legion of Honour. He made Suffolk his home, two of his sons serving as officers in the Suffolk Regiment and another as a Commander in the Royal Navy. His fourth son took Holy Orders. Hervey Lawrence lived to the age of 94, dying in 1975.

Finding homes for heroes

Unemployment, low pay and lack of decent housing were the big issues in the early post war years. In the summer of 1921 the number of unemployed topped two million with an equal number involved in pay disputes. Men turned to begging or took to the road, 171 tramps were seeking help at the Sudbury Workhouse in June, over a hundred more than in the same month the previous year. Each man was de-loused, if it was necessary, given a bath, a meal and a bed for the night, being expected to do a chore in recompense before he went on his way.

The housing situation led to the government's new Homes Fit for Heroes initiative requiring local authorities to provide housing at affordable rents with the help of government subsidy. In response, Sudbury Council put into motion a scheme that would eventually see dozens of modest homes built on the Wents, an area between York and Woodhall roads.

In addition, Suffolk County Council acquired land to divide into smallholdings for former soldiers, this included a large acreage on Sudbury's north eastern border that embraced much of the Chilton Hall estate. The land was parceled into 10-acre plots, each with a wooden bungalow that had begun life as an Army hut, and the new smallholders could borrow tools from a central store. In the years since, most of the land has been amalgamated into larger holdings either farmed by tenants or sold off for development. Some bungalows survive including a row on Chilton Hall Farm road, now mostly in private ownership.

1923 - Dorothy Hill with her son Peter and daughter Vivien outside the former army hut that was their happy home

WWI veteran George Hill was among the first smallholders. He had been discharged from the Army seriously ill with tuberculosis and without prospects other than a long spell of treatment in a TB sanatorium. The Homes Fit for Heroes scheme gave him a future with the necessary open air life, through tenancy of a smallholding on land that became part of the Homebase car park.

It was a complete change of life for George, a white-collar worker in his mid-20s, who knew nothing about farming, and even more so for his wife Dorothy, who had been privately educated and had worked in a West End store.

The couple's new life entailed hard physical labour and living without mains water and electricity in a home with an outside lavatory. When the well dried up, Dorothy had to carry water across the fields. But the couple set to, growing crops, keeping livestock and learning as they went along. They kept goats, pigs, chickens and bees, selling their produce to regular customers and at the gate.

Their produce also ensured their growing family was well fed and their son and six daughters thrived in the healthy country life. 'It was an idyllic childhood,' remembers Mrs Jean Gocher, one of their daughters.

George Hill ultimately bought the bungalow and after he retired in 1955, his eldest daughter Vivien Pryke and her husband Frank made it their family home for the next forty years.

1996 – Vivien and Frank Pryke leave the old family home

World War Two

Whatever the cost may be, we shall fight on the beaches, we shall fight on the landing grounds, we shall fight in the fields and in the streets, we shall fight in the hills: we shall never surrender.'

Winston Churchill, Prime Minister 1940-1945

Britain goes to war again
1939-1945

On the morning of 3rd September 1939, Prime Minister Neville Chamberlain told the nation in a radio broadcast that Britain was at war with Germany, the Nazi regime having ignored a demand to withdraw troops that had invaded Poland two days earlier. It was only 21 years since the end of 'the war to end all wars', as the 1914-1918 conflict had been called.

This time there was little bravado or obvious patriotism in Britain, memories of World War I were too sharp in the nation's memory. Many mutilated and traumatised survivors of the trenches were still very visible, as were the widows and hundreds of thousands of spinsters whose potential husbands had died in uniform. Above all was the realisation that sons, grandsons and nephews of the casualties of WWI would be called upon to resist Germany's second attempt to dominate Europe.

This war would be a very different conflict, fought in many more theatres with more powerful weapons and with all three services playing major roles, unlike the first World War when the Royal Flying Corps was not much more than a fledgling. Air power was now a potent threat and Britain's civilians would be on the front line to a far greater extent, since bombing would claim more than 60,000 lives.

The German military machine had been honed to conquer, Chancellor Adolf Hitler and his Nazi regime were determined to avenge Germany's humiliation in the First World War. In contrast Britain maintained an Army sufficient only to protect and police its Empire and was largely unprepared to do battle with such a powerful adversary.

The conflagration would spread across Europe, Russia, the Middle and Far East and Africa, involving Britain and Germany's empires and allies and eventually the United States. It would be six years before the fighting stopped at a cost of more than 73 million military and civilian deaths including those from the effects of war such as famine and disease. Britain's military losses at 382,000 would be less than half those of WWI and include the 60 names added to those on Sudbury War Memorial.

A call to arms in Suffolk

Britain did not fully address the reality that its Army was totally inadequate to deal with full-scale war until the Spring of 1939 when the Government conscripted fit and able men of 20 and 21 for six months training, and set out to double the strength of the Territorial Army. Full scale conscription

previous page : Infantry on exercise near Sudbury
left : From a daily newspaper 4 September, 1939

was not introduced until after the outbreak of war. The Territorials in the Sudbury Troop of a 58 Medium Regiment battery of the Royal Artillery, became part of the regular army on the first day of war, sharing the Drill Hall in Gainsborough Street with others from Haverhill. They used a property opposite for their cookhouse and ablutions, and a house called the Stone in Stour Street became the officers' mess. As the war progressed one regiment after another was billeted in buildings around Sudbury including the Moot Hall in Cross Street and what became the Dental Emporium.

Sudbury prepares to defend

Steps to protect the civilian population were already in place when Neville Chamberlain announced that the country was at war; gas masks had been issued, family air raid shelters provided in big cities and evacuation of children to the countryside was underway. On the first day of war Sudbury volunteers filled sandbags to protect the Town Hall and Police Station from bomb blast. The undulating wail of the air raid siren at the police station drifted across the town in a test run, leading to complaints from Ballingdon that it was not loud enough, and Father Gerard Moir, the Roman Catholic priest, went from street to street finding accommodation for evacuees arriving by double decker London bus.

Sudbury's Air Raid Precautions Service (ARP) had been set up a year earlier and would oversee the distribution of gas masks, those for children being made from red and blue rubber in the hope of making them less scary, and a hood with a large visor for babies.

Leslie Alston, shopkeeper and furniture manufacturer, was in overall charge of the town's ARP which had its base at Belle Vue, which had been a Red Cross Hospital in WWI. Chief Warden Bert Parsons had watchmaker and jeweller Ray Hills as his deputy, then there were two head wardens, each had a deputy, and finally the ordinary members. Wardens' duties included ensuring civilians took shelter during air raid warnings, and evacuating nearby property in the event of an unexploded bomb. Buildings designated as rest centres for those who might have to leave their homes, included Sudbury Senior School in Mill Lane, the Friends Meeting House in Friars Street and the crypt of the Roman Catholic Church. In time, public air raid shelters were built in Acton Square and

Vanners and Fennell silk mill ARP detachment

at the Melford Road end of North Street. The vaulted cellar beneath the Corn Exchange (now the town library) was reinforced to serve as another, and emergency reservoirs in Acton Square and behind the Police Station ensured a water supply for fire fighting should the mains be damaged.

> ## I remember . . .
>
> *'I was 17 when the ARP was set up and my job was to man the phones at Belle Vue. If a bomb dropped, the warden in that sector phoned in with the details and we would send an ambulance to take casualties to hospital if it was needed. The siren sounded on the day war broke out and we were ordered to put on our gas masks. We kept puffing and blowing because it seemed difficult to breathe, but we got used to them in the end.'*
>
> Betty Scrivener, born 1921

> ## I remember...
>
> *'We lived in Church Walk and they built an underground bomb shelter in Acton Square but we didn't use it because it was dark, damp and dreary. You had to take a candle. Then they built a brick one above ground on top of it and we didn't use that either because it was just as horrible. When there was an air raid we got under our table instead, a strong Suffolk kitchen table was as good as anything. We did have one use for the underground shelter. When it was frosty or snowed - we used to slide down the slope leading down into it.'*
>
> Sylvia Byham, born 1929, Sudbury Town Councillor

Put out that light!

Sudbury, like the rest of the country, went into a dark age as cities and towns were blacked out to make them less visible to enemy bombers both as a target and a navigation aid. There was no street lighting and windows had to be covered to prevent light escaping. Initially regulations forbade drivers from using headlights, but road deaths doubled and this order was modified to allow a two-inch-wide (5 cm) beam. Buses ran without interior lights, leading to chaotic situations. Posters urged those out after dark to wear something white, but there were so many minor accidents caused by people blundering about on moonless nights that the authorities issued small torches, the problem then being a shortage of batteries.

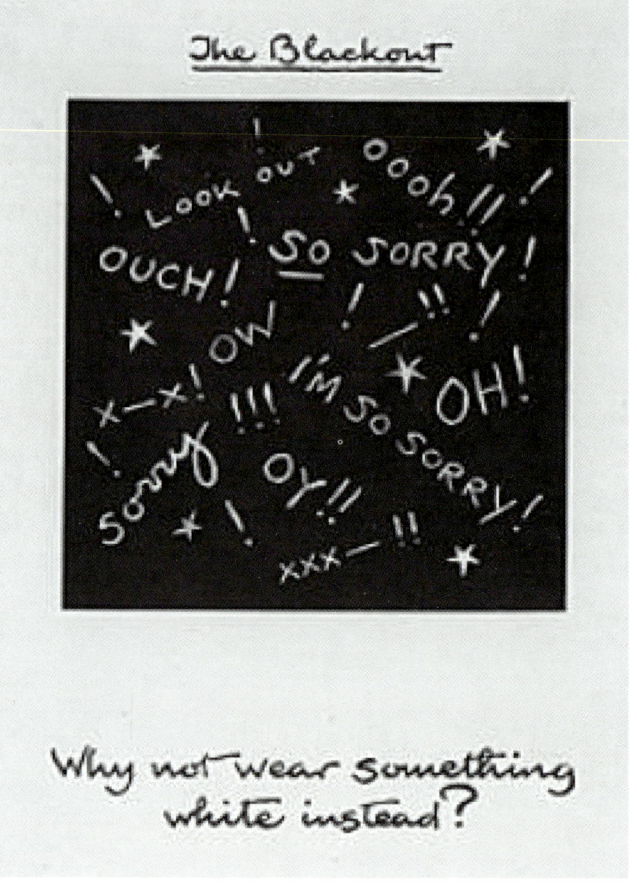

The long list of rules and regulations included identity cards and gas masks to be carried at all times at the risk of a fine. Showing a light after sunset was also an offence, even a chink seen around the edge of a window could lead to an air raid warden's knock on the door. Among those fined was the landlord at the Red Cow. Those too poor to buy blackout fabric used old rugs or even grey Army blankets left over from WWI.

The Madonna mystery

In late December The Times newspaper reported that one of Poland's most sacred treasures, the Black Madonna of Czestochowa, had been entrusted to the keeping of Sudbury's Roman Catholic priest Father Gerald Moir. The impression given was that the painting from the Jasna Gora monastery had been brought to England for safe keeping, but the truth is rather different. The Black Madonna handed over in that Christmas Eve ceremony - and still in the Roman Catholic Church on the Croft - is only a copy of the original. Perhaps it was a ruse to fool the Nazis that the Madonna had been smuggled out of the country.

The painting is reputed to be the work of St Luke and accredited with many miracles. For centuries pilgrims have flocked to pray before her including Pope John Paul II when he visited Poland during his Papacy.

Deeply involved in the event was Polish refugee Count Jan Balinski who spent the rest of his life in Sudbury working, both nationally and locally, to help his fellow countrymen and other refugees. He had fled with his wife Maria and four children as Soviet troops closed in on his country estate in eastern Poland. The family arrived in England with only their personal baggage, settling on the Croft, where the Countess opened a nursery school. In 1947 Count Balinski organised a visit by General Anders, Commander of the Polish Army in Britain, to a Polish student camp on Sudbury airfield.

The Count obdurately kept his refugee status in protest against Communist appropriation of his country, his estate and the Soviet policy of exiling landowners like him to Siberia. He and his wife were buried in Sudbury cemetery and their English-born daughter Caroline Lister still lives in the family home.

Pope John Paul II prayed before the Black Madonna

I remember . . .

'The nursemaid was taking me to school and the air raid siren sounded when we were nearly there. She turned and ran all the way back home with me and I remember feeling frightened and that the noise meant you had to do something quickly. Even now when I hear the sound of a siren it instantly takes me back to how I felt then.'

Michael Hills, born 1933, Sudbury's archivist

Dunkirk and fear of invasion 1940

A 'miracle of deliverance'

In January the Sudbury Territorial Gunners joined the British Expeditionary Force (BEF) in France ready to help protect our ally against any German invasion. The 1st Suffolks were already in position. With almost breakneck speed Germany invaded and overwhelmed Denmark and Norway in April, followed by Belgium and Holland in May. When Belgium capitulated the German Army swept into France, overwhelming the BEF and trapping 400,000 British and French troops in a pocket. So began the great retreat of our professional army, needed to be our island's defence against German invasion.

The Suffolk Gunners disabled their artillery weapons and marched ten miles to the coast on roads crowded with troops and refugees. Among them were brothers Jim and Joe Johnson, whose father Alfred, a disabled WWI veteran, had made and sold paper flowers to feed his family of twelve growing up in Gregory Street.

Saving Britain's Army

With Calais and Boulogne already in German hands, evacuating the BEF was concentrated on the small fishing port of Dunkirk which had a protective breakwater suitable for embarkation. But the size of the retreating French and British armies was so enormous that many troops waited for days on beaches and in sand dunes, being strafed and bombed by the Luftwaffe and shelled by the advancing German army. Rescue ships waited offshore in sight of the exhausted troops but unable to reach them. The trapped troops salvation was an armada of little ships - barges, fishing boats, tugs, ferries, lifeboats and private pleasure craft - that crossed the Channel to ferry them to transports offshore.

The exhausted troops waded out to meet them, patiently waiting in line for hours until it was their turn to board. There were more deaths in the struggle against wind, tide, cold, injury and attacks by the Luftwaffe. The Johnson brothers had been on the beach for four days before small boats came in at first light and began ferrying troops to two Dutch vessels. But the rising tide, whipped up by a fresh wind, was up to their shoulders by the time they were dragged into a small boat. Jim Johnson had saved his brother Joe's life by holding him up for five hours as they were buffeted by waves and current.

The Gunners were eventually landed at Margate pier, a small part of what Prime Minister Winston Churchill called 'a miracle of deliverance'. Against great odds 338,000 British and French troops had been rescued but more than 60,000 more had been killed, injured, taken prisoner or were missing, and Britain had lost six destroyers and the bulk of the Army's guns, and other equipment.

Death by explosion

Three years later the Johnson brothers were in the same gun crew fighting with the Eighth Army in North Africa. Thirty-year-old Bombardier Jim Johnson, who had saved his brother's life at Dunkirk, was killed when a jammed gun exploded. His wife Vilma at home in

Dunkirk

1940

'… great columns of men thrust out into the water among bomb and shell splashes. The foremost ranks were shoulder deep, in the command of young subalterns with their heads just above the water. As the front ranks were dragged aboard the boats the rear ranks moved up.'

Arthur Divine, crew on a small rescue craft

photo courtesy Imperial War Museum IWM NYP 068075

School Street, was a month away from giving birth to their third daughter. His brother Joe survived the explosion and the war, but three others with them died, including Sergeant Thomas Johnson, another Sudbury Territorial but not related to the Gregory Street family.

The Lancastria disaster

While Dunkirk was being hailed as a triumph, a great tragedy that would be hushed up was taking place on the Atlantic coast of France. With France on the verge of collapse, remaining British forces set out for the Atlantic coast. They were largely support units such as RAF ground crew, engineers and others in transport and communication roles. Waiting for them off the port of St Nazaire was the Cunard liner *Lancastria* in her role as a troopship and she must have been a welcome sight after their long trek to safety. The situation was so desperate that as many as 6,500 were taken on board including some civilians. That figure is one of several estimates, one as high as 9,000, although the truth will probably never be known.

The ship was still at anchor in the Loire estuary when the German Luftwaffe scored several hits including a bomb down the liner's single funnel into the engine room. It was a death blow, the troopship rolling over and sinking in 20 minutes with many trapped below decks, and hundreds clinging to the upturned hull.

French fishing boats, tugs and boats from other troopships rescued around 2,500, survivors telling of being machine gunned as they struggled in the oil-covered sea. The loss of life was so great that Winston Churchill imposed censorship fearing that news of the disaster would damage the country's morale at a time when invasion was imminent. The dead were listed as 'missing,' and survivors and rescuers were sworn to secrecy under the Official Secrets Act. The final report is under wraps until 2040, but the death toll is estimated as around 4,000, more than the combined total of those lost on the *Titanic* and the *Lusitania*, the disaster remaining the worst in Britain's maritime history.

Death of a boxer

Sudbury lost three men in the *Lancastria* disaster, one of them a local hero who died a hero. Lance Corporal Donald Theobald, serving with the Military Police, had been

above : The last moments of the Lancastria with hundreds clinging to her hull and others in the sea

top right : Lancastria as a Cunard liner

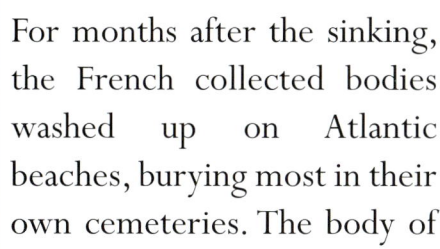

Boxing hero Donald Theobald

a successful amateur light heavyweight boxer before the war and was being tipped for a professional career. When the *Lancastria* went down he used his strength to save one man and died attempting to help others.

It was not until after the war that Herbert and Lily Theobald, living in Humphry Road, discovered that their 27-year-old son had been an unsung hero of the disaster. A Flight Sergeant Cherry wrote: 'Don and I were together on the ship when she got her final hit. I got a splinter in the leg and a few burns. Don got me up on the deck and then went back to help others who had been hurt. That was the last I saw of him as someone pushed me over the side and I swam round until I got picked up about an hour later. Don was the finest man I've met and I owe my life to him. If you ever hear any definite news would you please let me know.' There was none and Don Theobald is recorded as having died on the day of the sinking, his name listed on the Dunkirk memorial.

Another Sudbury man who died in the *Lancastria* disaster, was Corporal Charles Alfred Golding, 31, doubtless hoping for a speedy reunion with his wife Joyce at their home in Plough Lane. It is possible that he was among 800 RAF personnel who died when a bomb scored a direct hit on the hold where they were billeted. His name is among 20,000 RAF war dead lost without trace and commemorated on the Air Forces Memorial at Runnymede.

For months after the sinking, the French collected bodies washed up on Atlantic beaches, burying most in their own cemeteries. The body of 25-year-old Private Ernest Walter Smith, of the Royal Army Service Corps, came ashore at the village of Clion-sur-Mer, south of St Nazaire, where the mayor ordered trees to be felled for coffins in order to give him, and others, a decent burial in the community's own cemetery. Such an act would have been some comfort to his parents Walter and Annie Smith living in Upper East Street. His grave is one of more than 70 British military graves in the cemetery, mostly those of men from the *Lancastria*.

left: Charles Golding   right: Ernest Smith

The sea had already claimed the life of one Sudbury man. Leading Steward James Rowe, 27, died in April when enemy action sank *HMS Hunter* in icy Arctic waters off Narvik the day after a German force landed there. Only 35 of the destroyer's crew survived. Both Britain and Germany wanted control of the port which was an important link with Sweden's iron ore industry. James Rowe had joined the Royal Navy from school and was married. The wreck of *HMS Hunter* was found in 2008 and declared a war grave.

a pillbox on the Stour

Nazi Germany's invasion of France brought them to the Channel coast within 22 miles of England. Up to this moment the home front had been experiencing what became known as 'the Phoney War' in the absence of the expected air raids and airborne landings. Now coastal areas likely to be used as landing beaches were evacuated, a boys' school from Leiston moving in to share Sudbury Grammar School.

The supports of Ballingdon Bridge had already been packed with explosives and one hand rail removed to weaken the structure and ensure complete collapse. Somehow this anti-invasion measure was overlooked until the explosives were discovered by accident in the 1950s. Pill boxes guarded the Stour, part of a chain intended to be an important defence line against any invasion force driving in from the NE Essex Coast, two survive opposite Friars Meadow. Tank traps stood ready to be put in position in Ballingdon Street, and on other routes into the town. Road and rail station signs had been removed and town maps disappeared from shop counters.

'Dad's Army' keeps watch

Fear of invasion had led to the Government appealing in the Spring of 1940 for men aged 17 to 65 to join the Local Defence Volunteers, later re-named the Home Guard and immortalised in the long-running television comedy series Dad's Army. Thousands volunteered within the first 24 hours and there was an enthusiastic response in Sudbury. Some volunteers were WWI veterans, others too old or not deemed medically fit for the regular Army. They were joined by lads of 17 from the Army Cadet Force not due for conscription until they reached 18.

The fictional Walmington-on-Sea Home Guard was in some ways just a larger-than-life version of the real thing, as in the early days there was a severe shortage of weapons, ammunition, uniforms and equipment. At first volunteers wore a denim overall with an LDV armband, and a unit might be issued with an old sporting gun or two or an ancient carbine. Units drilled using broom handles, cudgels and anything else that came to hand, but none of it much use against German paratroopers. Eventually volunteers were issued with regular Amy uniforms and American weapons. They kept watch for enemy infiltration by day and night in Sudbury as the fear of an invasion mounted, and so did other companies in surrounding villages.

Sudbury's Home Guard

I remember . . .

'The Home Guard had a lookout post in the oak tree near the water tower at the top of Sheepshead Hill and the platform built on the spreading branches gave them a wide view of the Stour valley. They kept watch there every night in the early part of the war in case there was an invasion. The metal steps stapled in the trunk have all but disappeared.'

Reverend Tony Moore, born 1934

Invasion orders

The Government issued instructions for civilians on what they should do in the event of invasion, the military wanting to avoid a repeat of the situation in Belgium and France where fleeing civilians blocked roads, forming a human shield for the invaders.

Headed 'Stay where you are,' the leaflet is still chilling reading 70 years later. 'If you do not you will stand a very good chance of being killed,' it warns. 'The enemy may machine gun you from the air in order to increase panic, or you may run into enemy forces which have landed behind you.'

It instructs civilians to shelter, as if for an air raid, in a safe place in the house, 'or if you have a trench ready in your garden or field, so much the better.' It adds; 'Do not attempt to join in the fight. Behave as if an air raid were going on. The enemy will seldom turn aside to attack separate houses.'

Sudbury's radio hero

In July Sudbury lost its first known hero. RAF rear gunner Sergeant William Lillie was killed when his Sunderland flying boat was shot down over the North Sea with the loss of all the crew.

Almost everyone in Sudbury knew about Bill Lillie because a few months earlier BBC Home Service listeners had heard him describe how he had fought off six Luftwaffe Junker 88 fighter bombers attacking his Sunderland flying boat as it protected a North Sea convoy. They turned tail and fled after he shot down one and damaged another. There

Corporal Bill Lillie

could not have been prouder parents than Charles and Ethel Lillie living in Girling Street, especially as their 21-year-old son had been awarded the Distinguished Flying Medal.

Sudbury was delighted with its hero, the Mayor arranging an official party at the railway station to welcome him home on leave. But the modest former carpenter got wind of the plans, left the train at Bures and hitch-hiked home. He found Girling Street decorated in his honour with a greengrocer's chalk board reading: 'Germans afraid of Girling Street Boy. Good luck Corporal Bill Lillie'. His mother was not amused, she marched him to the railway station to meet the welcoming party.

A few months later Bill Lillie was dead but not forgotten. His memory lives on with a Sudbury street name - Corporal Lillie Close.

Later in the year Sudbury lost a second of young flyer. Grammar School boy Kenneth Ridgewell joined the RAFVR while a clerk with the Inland Revenue, learned to fly and was still only 18 when war came and he was called up. Six weeks after his 20th birthday, the now Sergeant Ridgewell was navigator on a Blenheim bomber that failed to return from a mission to aid the Greeks in their fierce struggle against Italian invaders. He was the only son of Frederick Ridgewell, foreman at the Halstead Co-op's Sudbury bakery. He and his wife Ada lived in Constable Road.

The Battle for Britain

By August Britain's civilian population was fairly blasé about the risk of bombing, so much so that on one particular market day, shoppers on Market Hill ignored yet another air raid warning, refusing to heed wardens' instructions to take cover. 'It was a disgrace,' one noted in his report. Planes had been spotted at a great height but then turned away. What the complacent shoppers did not know was that this day - August 15th - would see the heaviest fighting so far in the skies over Britain as the Luftwaffe fought for supremacy in preparation for Hitler's planned invasion. The RAF won the Battle of Britain, Hitler cancelling the German invasion plan two days after the battle reached its climax on September 15th.

The bombing of Sudbury

A Zeppelin airship raid in WWI had killed five people in Sudbury but in this war the town escaped very lightly, bombs dropped in and around the town causing little damage and only a few minor injuries. The first had damaged a brick wall and greenhouse in the Suffolk Road area - air raid wardens' reports did not give addresses. The list for late 1940 includes a bomb in a field at Acton Lane and an another that broke windows in Friars Street. These could have been ditched randomly by damaged Luftwaffe bombers returning from bombing strategic targets. In January 1941 an aircraft circled the town and dropped a high explosive bomb near Bulmer Road at Sudbury's southern boundary. A woman living at Brickfield Cottages was injured by flying glass and the blast broke windows in Ballingdon Street. That same month there are more reports of bombs on what is now the Springlands estate, another near a school - the report was non-specific. Yet another fell within a yard of a garden air raid shelter.

When it comes to counting the cost of bombing the two most unusual casualties were farmer Marshall's piglet and Mrs Sayers' groceries. The shopping came to grief when a bomb fell into a channel beside Sudbury Gas Works. It failed to explode but showered the surrounding area with sticky, black alluvial mud. Clods of it landed as far away as Station Road, one scoring a perfect bulls eye on the groceries in Mrs Sayers bicycle basket. 'She and my father laughed about it for a long time afterwards,' remembers her son John, who was to serve three terms as Mayor of Sudbury. 'We don't know what happened to the bomb, for all we know it is still down there somewhere'. The other casualty was Dick and Flo Marshall's piglet at Brickyard Farm off Newton Road, which was injured by a bomb that demolished a brick store and damaged their home.

1941 - More losses in the air and at sea

Eyes on the skies

When the RAF turned from defence to bombing Germany's industrial heartland, the Luftwaffe was intent on demoralising Britain's civilian population by bombing its cities. The Blitz reached a climax in May when 1,400 Londoners died in a raid on the capital by 1,000 Luftwaffe bombers and fighters. In Sudbury the Royal Observer Corps of local volunteers plotted the aerial activity, watching and listening for friend and foe from their post at the top of Constitution Hill. They were part of the network that served as the eyes and ears of Fighter Command, keeping watch in shifts around the clock and in all weathers from 1939 until long after VE day as Europe entered into the Cold War.

Radar installations tracked aircraft coming in from the sea, the Observer Corps taking over when they reached the coast. Their only aids were binoculars and a simple mechanical device to calculate the position and height of aircraft. Their skill at recognising aircraft by sight and sound played a major role in the deployment of fighter aircraft, air raid warnings and searchlight networks.

Sudbury Royal Observer Corps scanned the skies.
background: Aircraft silhouettes from the ROC handbook

The RAF brothers' bravery

The story behind a simple, white headstone in Sudbury cemetery is one of many family tragedies in WWII. It commemorates the two sons of Marcel and Mabel Fillmore, who were both killed at the same age while flying with the RAF. Their elder son, 23-year-old Sergeant Kenneth Fillmore, was air gunner on a Handley Page Hampden of 61 Squadron seriously damaged during a bombing raid on Cologne in the Rhineland. It limped back across the North Sea but crashed on landing killing all the crew. Shoppers knew him well as an assistant in the International Stores on the Market Hill and his father was chief goods clerk at the railway station. His brother Flying Officer Eric Fillmore worked as a railway clerk before following his brother into the RAF. History almost repeated itself in 1944 when the young Flying Officer was faced with getting his badly damaged Lancaster back from another bombing raid on Cologne, despite its fuel tanks being pieced in one wing and having only three engines. A landing wheel was damaged too but he put the Lancaster down safely. The feat earned him a Distinguished Flying Cross (DFC), the RAF medal for exceptional valour, courage and devotion to duty. Eric ended the war with the rank of Flight Lieutenant and stayed on in the RAF, but his luck ran out within a year. He crashed in 1946 while test flying a Supermarine Spitfire.

Guns and shelters

Sudbury had a surprise in 1941 when a hole excavated on the Market Hill turned out to be a gun emplacement for an anti-tank weapon issued to the Home Guard. The portable Blacker Bombard, a spigot mortar named after its inventor, could fire a 20lb (9kg) bomb 1,000 yards from stainless steel posts set in concrete at strategic points in the town. One mounting block opposite People's Park in Waldingfield Road became overgrown and survived into this century.

The air raid siren regularly wailed its warning but many preferred not to use their shelters. The outdoor Anderson type of curved corrugated iron sheets set in a pit and covered with earth, tended to turn into a pond in Sudbury's valley location. The Morrison indoor shelter, a box-like structure with a top of steel plates and removable mesh sides, was more popular but its size was a problem. It could only be used in a downstairs room because of its weight and being the size of a double bed did not leave much space in a typical living room. One Sudbury family solved the problem by putting their sofa on top of the shelter.

Women at war

In 1941 conscription brought single women aged from 20 to 30 into the war effort to free men for military service. Many women were already doing voluntary work in Sudbury including running the Women's Voluntary Service (WVS) canteen at the Town Hall which was popular with troops billeted in the town. Others with nursing skills served in the Voluntary Aid Detachment (VAD), based at Hardwicke House in Stour Street.

I remember. . .

'My father worked on the railway as well as being in the Sudbury Observer Corps. He would get so tired I have seen him fall asleep standing up. When they spotted an aircraft they would identify it then pass the information on to the next observer post in the direction it was heading. I used to test him by showing him an aircraft shape and he was always right., He was proud of doing the job because he knew that a lot depended on it.'

Terry Felton, born 1931,
son of ROC member George Felton

top : Women serving in Sudbury's Auxiliary Fire Service
bottom : Home Guard volunteers using spigot mortar

At sea with HMS Kelly

The war at sea caused more heartache in Sudbury in 1941. Leading Seaman Alfred Bareham, 23, died eight months after being severely injured in a torpedo attack on the destroyer *HMS Kelly*. His parents lived in Acton Lane. The ship was repaired and fought again but was sunk with the loss of half her crew during the evacuation of Crete. The wartime naval drama *In Which We Serve* is based on *HMS Kelly's* exploits, with Noel Coward in the role of her commander Lord Louis Mountbatten.

The battle for possession of the strategically important island of Crete cost thousands of lives both on land and at sea. The Germans suffered heavy casualties in an airborne landing, but managed to secure the airport and bring in reinforcements. The battle lasted for ten days before they overwhelmed the Allied defenders, taking more than 17,000 prisoners. The Royal Navy lost eight ships in addition to *HMS Kelly*, among them the cruiser *HMS Fiji*. Her crew fought off air attacks for two hours before she finally rolled over and sank. More than 500 survivors were picked up but among the 241 lost was 20-year-old Ordinary Seaman Emrys Vernon Bird who lived with his wife in Garden Row.

Another loss at sea

Former Suffolk policeman Able Seaman Joseph Moore, 32, died in December in the sinking of *HMS Chakdina*, a transport vessel torpedoed off the North African coast. On board were 380 British, Australian and New Zealand wounded being evacuated from Tobruk to Alexandria along with 100 German and Italian prisoners of war. The ship sank in three minutes, the wounded on stretchers in the hold stood little chance, particularly those in plaster casts. The destroyer *HMS Farndale* and the former Norwegian whaler *HMS Thorgrim* pulled about 200 men from the sea, but the Sudbury seaman was not among those saved.

Brought up in Sudbury, Joseph Moore had been recalled to the Royal Navy from the reserve having served for seven years before joining the Suffolk Police. He sailed on Christmas Day 1939 and it was the last time his wife Dorothy and their two children would see him. His parents, railway worker Robert Moore and his wife Bessie, living at Gardenside in Croft Road, lost two of their three sons in the war. Joseph's younger brother Jimmy died in 1943 as a prisoner of war in the Far East.

Among those rescued from the *Chakdina* was Generallieutnant Johann von Ravenstein, the first German General to be captured in the war. New Zealand forces had taken him prisoner outside Tobruk on his way to Afrika Korps headquarters.

On the Home Front Sudbury lost one of its best known characters when William Barnes, popular manager of the County Cinema, died suddenly while home on leave from the Royal Army Pay Corps. The veteran from the 1914-18 war had volunteered to serve even though he was in his 40s. He had came to Sudbury as landlord of the Royal Oak and then expanded his business and community activities to include the cinema, a seat on the Town Council, and the office of secretary to the forerunner of the town's Chamber of Commerce.

Capture at Singapore and RAF losses
1942

5th Suffolks in mass surrender

The history of the 5th Suffolks in WWII almost mirrored the Battalion's experience in the First World War; a long period of training followed by a voyage to a place few of them had even heard of, and then extreme suffering and death. In the 1915 it was the trauma of Gallipoli, and in 1942 the Fall of Singapore which resulted in thousands of Allied troops dying as prisoners.

As in WWI, there were many men from Sudbury and the surrounding villages in the Battalion. After training for almost two years they sailed in late October 1941 from Liverpool on the transport ship *Reina del Pacifico* as part of the 54th Infantry Brigade. It was to be a three-month-long journey to an unknown destination, via Nova Scotia, Trinidad, and Cape Town, to cut the risk of U-boat attack, reaching Bombay a few days after Christmas.

The war had taken a dramatic turn during their journey, the United States having joined the Allies following the shock Japanese attack on Pearl Harbour. The Battalion reached Singapore on 29 January to find the docks under attack by Japanese aircraft and the remnants of the RAF being evacuated. Two days later the Japanese crossed the causeway separating the island from Malaya and finally overwhelmed its defences. The 5th Suffolks had travelled 20,000 miles only to be captured in the largest surrender of British troops in history.

Two Sudbury men died in the fighting, Private Reginald Cansdale, 25, of the 5th Suffolks was killed on the day the island fell to the Japanese. He was one of the few who had previous experience of action, having fought in France with the 1st Suffolks and been rescued from Dunkirk. His arrival home then must surely have been a great relief to his mother Mary, living in Constable Road, since his father had been killed at Passchendaele in 1917. This time she was to wait until the autumn of 1945 to be officially notified that her son was dead. Twenty-one-year old George Risby of the Cambridgeshire Regiment was also killed defending the island. He was the son of George and Grace Risby living in Cross Street.

Japanese infantry hold men of the Suffolk Regiment at gunpoint

A launch for a gunboat

'Save, save, save' was a constant mantra on the Home Front, with special week-long events to encourage investment in Government savings stamps, bonds and certificates to fund the war effort. But there was an underlying purpose too - it limited the population's ability to spend on goods made with precious raw materials. Warship Week in February was one of these special savings drives, launched jointly by the Sudbury Council and the now defunct Melford Rural District Council. The local target was to achieve an extra £75,000 invested in National Savings, a tidy sum then but the equivalent in the present retail price index would be more than £2.5 million.

Barnsley had raised £1 million to adopt two destroyers, but Sudbury and Melford's target had to be within their means and the vessel in the town's sights was the river gunboat *HMS Scarab*. She was elderly, a veteran of patrols on the Yangtze river, and designed for the days when native unrest in a corner of Britain's Empire led to the command 'Send a gunboat.'

Local enthusiasm grew for the project. Villages drew up their own programme of activities to help reach the target. Saving stamps were offered as prizes in competitions, and ticket money paid for entry to an event would be given back in the same form.

The Sudbury organisers launched Warship Week with a parade from the Croft to Market Hill headed by the pipes of the London Scottish Regiment troops billeted in the town, and followed by the Home Guard, civil defence organisations and Army Training Cadets. Flags fluttered and a slogan on a banner across the Town Hall urged 'The signal is save.' A Royal Navy captain took the salute followed by the inevitable speeches. Activities included dances, variety concerts, boxing and bridge tournaments and a parade of mechanised vehicles from Long Melford to the Market Hill. Traders entered into the spirit with window displays of photographs, Alston's in the Old Market Place displayed a 500lb bomb and a Browning gun. The result of all this activity was £144,000 in extra savings, almost enough to adopt the gunboat twice over.

Scarab goes to war

Sudbury and Melford's gunboat fought in the cauldron of the Mediterranean, mainly shelling enemy-held territory with her two six-inch guns, and supporting landings in Sicily and Italy. Perhaps her finest moment was in August 1944 when the Allies landed a huge force on the French Riviera, liberating two thirds of France in 30 days. Scarab and two other ships had earlier bombarded further along down the coast, successfully convincing the Germans that this was the chosen area for landings. After the war, Scarab was loaned to the Burmese Navy and finally sold for scrap in 1948. Sudbury Museum Trust has the carved wooden shields the ship presented to the two local councils.

top : HMS Scarab at war
above left : motif on the commemorative shields
bottom : Pre-war Scarab on the Yangtse

The toll in Bomber Command

Almost a third of Sudbury's dead in the Second World War served in the RAF, mostly as bomber crew. The chances of surviving in Bomber Command was calculated as being less than that of an infantry officer in WWI. On long missions over occupied Europe they faced heavy ground fire, particularly around the industrial cities of the Ruhr, as well as attacks by Luftwaffe fighters and the risk of accidental collisions. Altogether 55,000 of those who flew with Bomber Command were lost - a death rate of 44 per cent - and more than 13,000 aircraft were shot down, wrecked in crashes or were written off due to damage.

In the Spring of 1942 Ben Dove and Findon Row, both sergeants in the RAFVR, were lost just two weeks apart, their Wellingtons from 12 Squadron based at Binbrook in Lincolnshire, failing to return from missions over Europe. Ben was 22 and had plans to climb the ladder at the Borough Surveyor's office and to marry his fiancée. His parents, Town Councillor Albert Dove and his wife Jennie clung to the hope that he might be alive, but eighteen months later his body was washed ashore in Holland and buried in Amsterdam.

Two week's after Ben Dove was shot down, the news arrived that another Wellington had gone missing with 27-year-old Sergeant Findon Row aboard. His parents, Herbert and Margaret living in York Road were never to see him again. He is commemorated on the Air Forces Memorial at Runnymede to those who have no known grave. Not long after their deaths 12 Squadron took part in a 1,000 aircraft raid that reduced much of Cologne to rubble.

Disease and 'friendly fire'

Two soldiers named on Sudbury War Memorial fought in the North Africa campaign to defend access to Middle East oil and the Suez Canal. The Germans captured Gunner Frank Bear of the Royal Artillery in June, the month in which Field Marshall Rommel's Army took the all-important Tunisian port of Tobruk and its defenders. The loss of the 35,000 Allied troops and their equipment was a major setback for the war effort.

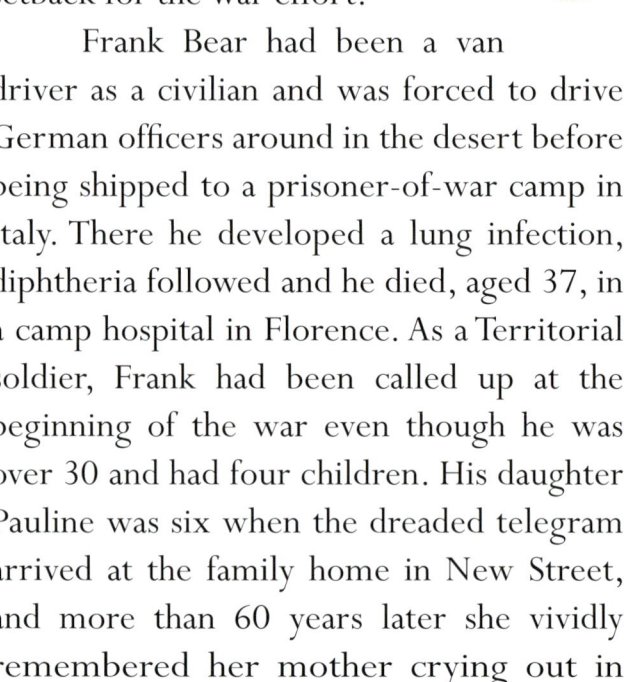

Frank Bear

Frank Bear had been a van driver as a civilian and was forced to drive German officers around in the desert before being shipped to a prisoner-of-war camp in Italy. There he developed a lung infection, diphtheria followed and he died, aged 37, in a camp hospital in Florence. As a Territorial soldier, Frank had been called up at the beginning of the war even though he was over 30 and had four children. His daughter Pauline was six when the dreaded telegram arrived at the family home in New Street, and more than 60 years later she vividly remembered her mother crying out in shock as she stood reading it.

below : Group of WWII British aircrew

Former Sudbury plumber Sapper Edward Wordley of the Royal Engineers was taken prisoner in Libya. As the war progressed, he was moved from a prison camp in Italy to another in Germany and finally to the former Czechoslovakia. He was killed, aged 29, on May 8th, 1945, the day the war officially ended. His parents, Henry and Kate Wordley living in Cross Street, were told he was killed by a shell fired by a Russian tank just before the camp was liberated.

Edward Wordley

The boy sailors

HMS *Ganges*, the Royal Navy's training establishment on the Shotley peninsular, was a magnet for boys who wanted to escape Sudbury's small town existence, and some died at sea in WWII. Able Seaman Reginald French was lost when a U-boat submarine sank the destroyer *HMS Veteran* engaged on convoy escort duty protecting merchant ships carrying armaments, raw materials, needed to feed Britain's population and its war effort. Packs of U-boats hunted the convoys and *HMS Veteran* was picking up survivors from two American ships when the fatal torpedo struck. The destroyer sank quickly with the loss of her entire crew of 159 together with those she had rescued. More than 5,000 Allied ships were sunk in the North Atlantic during the course of the war.

Four weeks later another Ganges boy sailor, Ordinary Seaman George Henderson, became another victim of a U-boat aged only 17, he was serving on *HMS Phoebe*, torpedoed off the Congo in West Africa. A Marine serving on the cruiser later recalled: 'A lot of boy seamen died. Their mess deck was below that of the Marines and took the full force of the explosion. The sail maker seeing to a boy for burial, was crying his eyes out.' The lad from Newmans Road, Sudbury, was among more than 40 fatalities.

Albert Heard saw action as a teenager on board *HMS Cumberland* at the Battle of the River Plate in 1939. The Royal Navy trapped the damaged German pocket battleship *Admiral Graf Spee* in the neutral harbour of Montevideo in Uruguay and waited outside, eager to exact retribution for the nine merchant ships she had sent to the bottom of the Atlantic. But the German captain scuttled his ship rather than surrender. Five years later Albert Heard was a Petty Officer when an infected appendix indirectly led to his death. After surgery he was re-assigned to *HMS Bullen*, and in 1944 he and 70 others,

George Henderson

I remember . . .

'My mother volunteered me as a casualty in a defence exercise in Ballingdon Street, I was eight at the time. I think it was mainly for the Home Guard but other defence organisations were there. Real tear gas was used and we were all coughing. I was lying on the pavement and bandaged up for a head injury and my arm put in a splint. Some of the people lying around were covered up as if they were dead. I was finally carried away on a stretcher. It was good fun at the time.'

Barry Wall, born 1934, local historian

Albert Heard

went down with the frigate when she it was torpedoed by a U-boat off north west Scotland. He was still only 22. His original ship *HMS Cumberland* survived the war. It was a double blow for his family, Albert's cousin, 20-year-old Charles Heard, had been killed two months earlier serving with the Royal Artillery in Holland.

Leading Seaman Alexander Pearce suffered leg wounds on D-Day in June 1944 as he manned a Bofors gun on a ship supporting the largest seaborne invasion in history when almost three million Allied troops crossed the English Channel to land in France. He was invalided out of the Navy but re-enlisted the following year joining *HMS Goodall*. In April 1945 the American-built frigate was sunk by a U-boat in the icy waters off the northern coast of the Soviet Union while escorting a convoy. Only 44 of the crew of 156 survived and 21-year-old Alex Pearce was not among them. His parents living at Park Lodge, Newton Road, learned of his death three days after V E Day in May, 1945. He was the last of the nine Sudbury sailors who died in the war and *HMS Goodall* was the last Royal Navy ship sunk in the European theatre of war.

Death in the Stour

Twenty-year-old Harry Everitt drowned close to home in an accident on the River Stour during a joint civil defence and military exercise in September. He was leading a first aid party ordered to deal with a supposed casualty on the Essex side of the river. Ballingdon Bridge was in 'enemy' hands so he and a fellow first aider hailed two members of the RAF in a canoe. One agreed to ferry them across the river but the overloaded canoe capsized and Harry Everitt drowned. The inquest into his death was told that he was unable to swim. The coroner ruled that he was a casualty of war in the fullest sense. He had in fact just received his call up papers for military service.

Nurse's dedication

Nurse Connie Prigg paid a high price for devotion to her Royal Navy patients. She ignored her own pain to continue nursing until the hip she had damaged in a fall was beyond repair. Despite years in hospital she was bedridden until her death more than 30 years later, but regularly worshipped at St Gregory's Church while lying in a long basket. Connie had the fateful fall while she was nursing at *HMS Watchful*, a shore establishment at Great Yarmouth, before that she was at *HMS Ganges* at Shotley. She was born at the Black Boy on Market Hill, and after her parents deaths when she was only a teenager, she and her life-long friend Kathleen Backhouse ran the nearby West Suffolk Hotel together.

Nurse Prigg, centre, at HMS Ganges

In which we serve

The war put many into uniform on the Home Front. As well as the Home Guard, ARP service and the Observer Corps, the uniformed ranks in Sudbury included the enlarged ambulance service and the Auxiliary Fire Service. Women worked alongside men in most of these essential services, although their roles were often confined to clerical work and manning the organisation's telephones.

Sudbury's historic photo archive holds photographs from the war years which capture the faces of some who donned uniforms to fight on the Home Front.

Sudbury Auxiliary Fire Brigade stationed at Chilton House in Newton Road

Women in Dad's Army

Early in 1943 the War Office authorised the Home Guard to enrol women as auxiliaries and large numbers joined, working mainly as signals clerks and drivers. It was always a sore point that they were denied a uniform, their only insignia being a badge, but by unrecorded means many managed to acquire one. Their position as soldiers was, however, defined under international law. Home Guard Commanders were given instructions that ensured women auxiliaries would be entitled to the same treatment as a serving soldier should they be taken prisoner.

above: Women auxiliaries in Sudbury Home Guard
below: Sudbury Ambulance personnel based at Belle Vue during the war years

More bombers lost and rationing bites

Drama above the North Sea

Getting a badly damaged bomber home across the North Sea was a frequent ordeal for crews of Bomber Command. Flight Lieutenant Verdun Ashley Scott won the Distinguished Flying Cross in 1942 for his achievement in nursing his aircraft back after being shot up returning from a bombing raid on the German industrial city of Bremen. The citation tells the story: 'The petrol tanks were pierced and the hydraulics shot away, causing the undercarriage to drop. Despite this Pilot Officer Scott flew on and although height was gradually lost whilst flying over the North Sea, the English coast was safely reached and he effected a masterly forced landing in a field. Throughout the operation, this officer displayed skill and judgment of a high degree.' He was promoted flight lieutenant the same year. In September 1943 he was killed, aged 27, with all his crew when his Wellington bomber crashed taking off from an airfield in Algeria on a mission to hunt U-boats causing heavy losses among Allied shipping in the Mediterranean.

He had learned to fly in Canada under the Commonwealth Air Training Plan, and received his pilot's 'wings' from the Duke of Kent, youngest brother of King George VI, to the obvious pride of his widowed mother Ethel living in Upper East Street. She had raised her son alone following her husband's early death. His unusual first name commemorated the WWI battle of Verdun fought by the Germans and French in the year he was born, it being commonplace for a second name to be the one intended for everyday use. Before enlisting he had at one time been a clerk at the Walnuttree Institution, which was the successor to the Sudbury Workhouse.

The most senior RAF officer named on the War Memorial, Squadron Leader John Flowerdew, was killed in May during a bombing raid over Germany while flying a Halifax of 102 Squadron based at Pocklington in Yorkshire. He had joined the RAF well before the war and created a stir in the mid-1930s by making an emergency landing in a field at Chilton. His Commanding Officer was apparently highly suspicious since he put his biplane down conveniently close to his home, Chilton House in Newton Road once occupied by the Armes family. The Squadron Leader is commemorated on the Air Forces Memorial at Runnymede to flyers who have with no known grave.

Leading Aircraftman Jack Cresswell's role in the RAFVR was less glamorous than that of aircrew, but just as essential. When he died in February at the age of 22, he was an armourer responsible for loading aircraft with the weapons of war at a RAF station in Yorkshire. The former Sudbury Hotspur player's funeral was held at St Gregory's Church where he had been a choirboy. Before the war he worked for printers Marten and Son on Market Hill and was engaged to be married.

The Distinguished Flying Cross
right : Cecil Beaton's portrait of pilot and co-pilot in a Wellington bomber

Food rations cut

Food rationing began in 1940 and allowances were gradually reduced and the number of rationed foods increased, until even the humble sausage was rationed in 1943. For example, in January 1940 an adult was allowed 8oz (226g) of butter a week but this was reduced to 2oz (56g), and the cheese ration was pared from 8oz to 1oz (28g), which was just enough for a mouthful. A typical weekly ration included one egg and two pints of milk. Allowances varied from time to time according to available stocks, and these reflected the number of ships surviving the transatlantic crossing because Britain was reliant on more than two thirds of its food being imported.

Food rationing continued long after the war. Gainsborough Street butcher Tom Cook displays a typical meat ration for a week in 1951 - Festival of Britain year. It amounted to one chop, or the equivalent in beef, or a 4oz (113g) piece of steak, all with a small amount of corned beef.

Every man, woman and child was registered with specific retailers who rubber stamped coupons in their ration books to show they had been supplied. Meat, tea, jam, eggs, biscuits, milk, dried fruit, tinned goods, sugar, soap, coal, clothing and petrol were all rationed as the war progressed, and the situation was even worse afterwards when bread and potatoes were added to the list as the Allies struggled to feed the starving of war-torn Europe. But prices were controlled and few went hungry in comparison with the

Food rationing continued long after the war and this one from 1953 was registered with grocer E W King on Market Hill and Dewhurst the butcher in King Street

I remember...

'There were three of us children and we lived on rabbit. My father [George Parker] was the groundsman at the Grammar School and he used to catch them on the playing field up Acton Lane. We had a pig too at my aunt's house in Inkerman Row that stood where the conservatory of Playford Court is now. We used to save our scraps for the pig and just before Christmas it was taken to the butcher's and the meat shared out four ways in the family.'

Sylvia Byham, born 1929

pre-war years when malnutrition was not uncommon. Sudbury people fared better than city dwellers because they were able to draw on produce from the surrounding countryside. In addition, the Government urged the population to 'Dig for Victory' and every available piece of land, including parks and garden lawns, was turned over to producing food.

Children craved sweets because the ration was the equivalent of only 2oz (56g) a week and there were few other snacks. It was good for children's teeth but not for their appetite for sweet things, and a favourite substitute was a stringy piece of liquorice root chewed to release the flavour.

Food retailers had to register to obtain supplies, and Government stocks were kept at both Vanner's Gregory Mills and at Arlington's in Cornard Road. The old library in North Street (later the site of Argos) was converted into a British Restaurant that served good, cheap meals that did not count as rations. Children from North Street primary school were taken there for lunch and free milk was provided in schools. The Ministry of Food issued condensed orange juice and cod liver oil for under twos.

I remember...

'We did all sorts of thing to make the food go round. I used to take the cream off the milk and shake it until it turned into butter. There would be just enough for one slice of bread. Eggs were on ration so I bought day-old chicks in the market. They all died except one and that was a cockerel. When Christmas came we gave him away because we couldn't bear to eat him'.

Winifred Cole, born 1910

The British Restaurant in North Street

Runaway lorry kills Inspector

There was a tragedy on the Home Front in September when Sudbury Police Inspector Ronald Pooley died under the wheels of a runaway ballast lorry at the junction of Newton Road and King Street. There is a story that he was killed trying to save the life of an elderly widow, but that is not supported by evidence given at the inquest.

Keeping the troops warm

In the cruel Russian winter of 1942/3 thousands of German troops froze to death during the siege of Stalingrad. This morale-boosting publicity photograph (below) taken on the Croft, celebrated the work of more than 100 local women who made battledresses for the Army at a former Vanner's silk factory in Girling Street. After the war the Rego company wanted to switch production to making clothing for the civilian market but was unable to recruit sufficient labour. Vanners resumed production there until the mid 1990s. The substantial range of buildings was finally demolished in 1999 and Aldi supermarket built on the site.

More uniforms on parade with members of Sudbury Police and Fire Brigade leading the judge's procession on the first day of Quarter Sessions

Pioneer long-distance flyer Jean Batten accepted an invitation to launch Sudbury Wings for Victory savings week in 1943. In the 1930s the New Zealander was more famous than Britain's heroine Amy Johnson, having broken her records for solo flights.

In 1937 at the age of 28, Jean Batten had flown her single-engine Percival Gull from Australia to England in five days 18 hours, faster than anyone else of either sex. She had already made record-breaking flights from England to South America and from England to New Zealand. Auckland airport is named after her, but when she died on the island of Majorca in 1982 she was buried in a pauper's grave because nobody knew she was the famous flyer.

When rail was king

Trains ran through Sudbury station night and day for much of the war and its goods yard played an important role in the war effort. At that time Sudbury had rail links to Cambridge and Bury St Edmunds, as well to the Norwich-Liverpool Street line, and in 1943 this was used by freight trains loaded with bomb damage rubble for building USAAF airfields at Sudbury and Wormingford. Once operations began in at Wormingford in November that year, two more ran daily on the same route carrying high-octane fuel for the fighter group based there. From February 1944 the line was in operation 24 hours a day for troop trains, as well as for those moving freight, and signalmen worked 12-hour shifts.

The single track line began the most dramatic period of activity in its history when the USAAF 486th Bomb Group arrived at the newly-completed airfield at Chilton in 1944. Tanker trains loaded with aircraft fuel were shunted into Sudbury's then extensive sidings, ready for being transported onward by road. Three or four times a week freight trains delivered the enormous quantities of bombs to Long Melford. Up to 100 tons of bombs were needed for each mission flown from the base together with about 100,000 gallons of fuel. The line also serviced other USAAF bases.

American servicemen using Sudbury station for off-duty trips to London, Cambridge and Colchester were charmed by the diminutive size of the locomotives in comparison with their own monsters, and by the mid-Victorian buildings. But others saw the station in unhappy circumstances. Every Sunday ambulances connected with a hospital train that took seriously wounded aircrew either onward to major hospitals, or to be flown back to the United States. The traffic was in the other direction after both D-Day in June 1944 and the Battle of the Bulge in the winter of 1944/45, when casualties from both arrived at Sudbury to be treated at the American 136 Station Hospital at Acton Place.

It seems that the railway station held a special place in the Americans' affections, since USAAF veterans on sentimental journeys often go back there. Sadly they are disappointed, as the cosy little Victorian structure was demolished in about 1987, having served for some time as the town museum.

The once-thriving goods yard at Sudbury

Friendly invaders join the fray 1944

Sudbury welcomes the USAAF

The biggest single impact on the town was the friendly invasion by the 486th Bomb Group, part of the USAAF Eighth Army which raided targets in occupied Europe from air bases in Eastern England.

In April 1944 their bombers began touching down at a newly-constructed airfield on the plateau alongside Waldingfield Road that became variously known as Sudbury, Chilton, Great Waldingfield and even Acton airfield though the major part of it lies in Chilton parish. Before long it was a small town of 3,000 men within two miles of Sudbury's Market Hill. Since the town's population was only about 7,000, their presence changed life and lives.

With their smart uniforms, strange accents and colloquialisms, they might have come from another planet as far as the locals were concerned, and they too found the Suffolk customs and speech difficult at times.

These were the days before the post-war London overspill estates brought Thames Estuary English to Sudbury. The American airmen took to Sudbury and the town soon reciprocated by welcoming them into their homes. Women particularly liked their politeness, such as the 'yes, please Ma'am' and 'thank you Ma'am' that accompanied their pleasure at being offered a chair by a warm fire together with a home-cooked meal, however frugal it was due to food rationing. These homely comforts meant a lot to men living in an all-male world far from home. In return there would often be a gift of tinned peaches or some other treat sold on the base, and local women benefited from jobs at the American Red Cross Service Club where the Post Office now stands. Others supplemented their income by taking in the Americans' washing, their fast, efficient service being much appreciated in contrast to the military laundry.

above : The American Red Cross Service Club in East Street
right : US planes flying over Sudbury Station

The Yanks come to Sudbury

'The sky over eastern England was as full of traffic as Piccadilly Circus - there was never a time, except during the worst weather, when one could not count a score, fifty or a hundred aircraft coming, going, circling in small formations.'

from *Here We are Together* by Robert S Arbib,
a USAAF staff sergeant based in Suffolk

1944

There could be problems when friendships became too close between an American GI and a local woman whose husband was away at the war. At least one such fracas ended up in court although military and local police kept a close eye on likely trouble spots.

There were frequent dances, baseball demonstrations, tennis matches, children's parties on the base and lots of drinking and romancing. The Americans loved Sudbury's old pubs and many a time they managed to drink one dry. The friendly invasion was near heaven for small boys who watched the real cops and robbers of war being played out with giant aircraft, made friends with their crews and collected souvenirs. The Americans were ever generous, especially where children were concerned, and a small boy's request of 'got any gum, chum?' usually resulted in the prized gift. But the business of war was ever audible and visible with the sight and sound of their aircraft coming and going. When 50 or more bombers ran up their four engines in preparation for a major raid, the ground shook in Great Waldingfield and Chilton and the roar could be heard in Sudbury. They would then take off at one minute intervals.

There were many sad farewells when airmen went back to a home posting in the USA after completing their 30 missions. The total who died has been generally accepted as 400 but new research suggests the total is fewer. The average age of a bomber crew was only 21. After Victory in Europe Day in May, 1945, the 486th flew peace missions carrying food to the starving Dutch population and ferrying British prisoners of war back from Germany. They finally left for home in July and August. There was genuine sadness in Sudbury at the loss of friends, and even tears among young women although some became GI brides and crossed the Atlantic

It was not the last chapter in the story of the most extraordinary invasion in Britain's history, one which was incomprehensible to local men who went away to war before the airfield was built and then came back to find it deserted. For more than 60 years after the war men of the 486th continued to return,

this page : US servicemen relaxing at the American Service Red Cross Club
next page : life at the base, north of Sudbury

some with their grandchildren, in order to refresh memories of the most intensively-lived period of their youth. They have always been given the warmest of welcomes with both Sudbury and Great Waldingfield offering hospitality and entertainment.

In 2009 Sudbury unveiled a special tribute to them by adding a permanent feature to the town's Heritage Centre and Museum which relates the story of the friendly invasion by the 486th, its relationship with the town and lists the names of those who did not go home. An associated website enables the story of the 486th and Sudbury to be read anywhere in the world. It was a timely decision on the part of the museum trustees, since the 21-year olds of 1944 are in their mid 80s and their numbers thinning fast. Before long only the written memories and the memorials will remain - the rest will be history.

above : USAAF Final parade outside Sudbury Town Hall before going back to the States
left : Plaque outside the Town Hall
right : The 486th Commemoration stone adjoining Sudbury War Memorial

A bridge too far

In September the 486th put up 56 bombers to support Operation Market Garden, the airborne mission intended to capture bridges across the Rhine in order to shorten the war. The story of the operation is told in the epic *A Bridge too Far*, and the name of the town of Arnhem is linked with one of the most dramatic episodes in WWII.

The B-17s crossed the North Sea to Holland in formations of six, each loaded with thirty fragmentation bombs, and with orders to attack flak batteries at a bridge south of Rotterdam. Mission accomplished they turned for home, passing wave upon wave of aircraft towing gliders loaded with paratroopers heading for the Rhine.

The Sudbury-based flight of bombers returned safely, but the Allied airborne force withdrew after nine days of savage fighting that cost more than 8,000 casualties. Among them was Private Harry Warburton, 31, of the 1st Parachute Regiment, who lived in Friars Street with his wife and young son. His regiment landed to the west of Arnhem and was reduced to 100 as it fought to reach troops cut off at the bridge. Harry Warburton was at first reported missing, and then as killed in action on the last day of the operation. His name is recorded on the Groesbeek Memorial near Nijmegan to those who have no known grave.

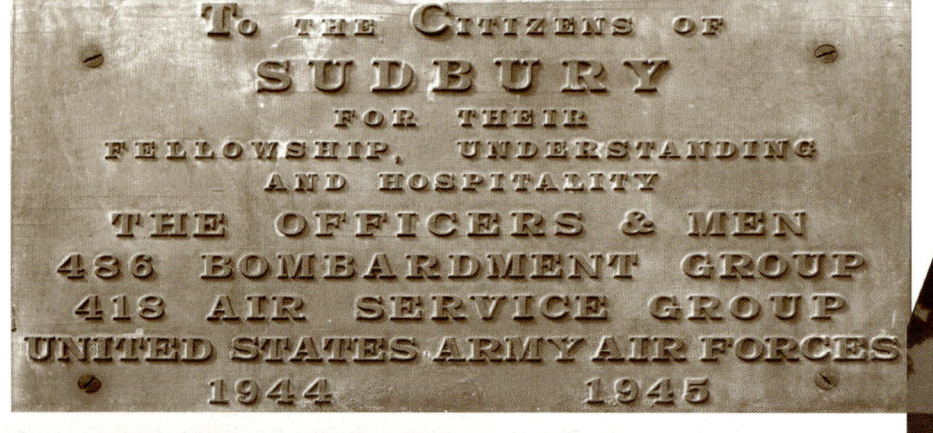

A boyhood friendship

In 1995 an American WWII flying jacket was presented to Sudbury Town Council. The ceremony was the outcome of a friendship between a young USAAF air gunner based with the 486th at Sudbury airfield and a local schoolboy Ted Filer that was to last more than 65 years.

The flyer was former air gunner Ray Garrett, (later treasurer of the 486th Bomb Group Association) and the schoolboy was Ted Filer, a budding artist who became chief designer at Stephen Walters' silk mill. As a 14-year-old he painted a B-17 bomber and other motifs on the back of Garrett's jacket. It is now part of the museum collection.

At the age of 79, Ted Filer's recollects his schooldays' friendship with two of the USAAF crews. 'I was 13 when I saw my first bomber close to. It was a few days after the Liberators had arrived and I had gone up to the airfield on my bike. It taxied up to where I was standing by a hole in the hedge, its engines roaring. I was thrilled, I'd never been so close to anything so large and it towered over me. The crew saw me standing there and called me over to have a look inside.'

Ted made friends with the crew and another in Scorpio squadron. 'I used to do errands for them so nobody minded me and other boys like Roley Andrews being on the base. If an MP (military police) or anyone else asked what we were doing we just told them who we were going to see. The Americans were so friendly, they really liked having us boys around and we had some great times. They took me to their mess hall and to the base cinema and they taught us boys to play baseball. I asked John Mroz, who was in one of the crews, if he could get me a watch if I gave him the money. He took his own off and gave it to me as a birthday present - I was then almost 14. It still works and I wear it sometimes. I've got other souvenirs of those days including three silver pilot's wings'.

Ted Filer kept in touch with some of his flyer friends after the war and two returned in 1987 for the unveiling of the 486th memorial, outside St Gregory's churchyard. Roley Andrews dedicated much of his life to collecting photographs, documents and other 486th memorabilia, most of which he generously passed on to other collections.

above left : Fifty years on: the schoolboy, Ted Filer, right, the flyer, Ray Garrett, left, and Sudbury's then Mayor Michael Gould wearing the WWII jacket

below : Ted Filer's friends included Pilot Frank Farrell's crew. By 2009 he had died along with most of his crew including gunner Paul Maza, right, wearing a jacket that Ted painted with his tally of missions.

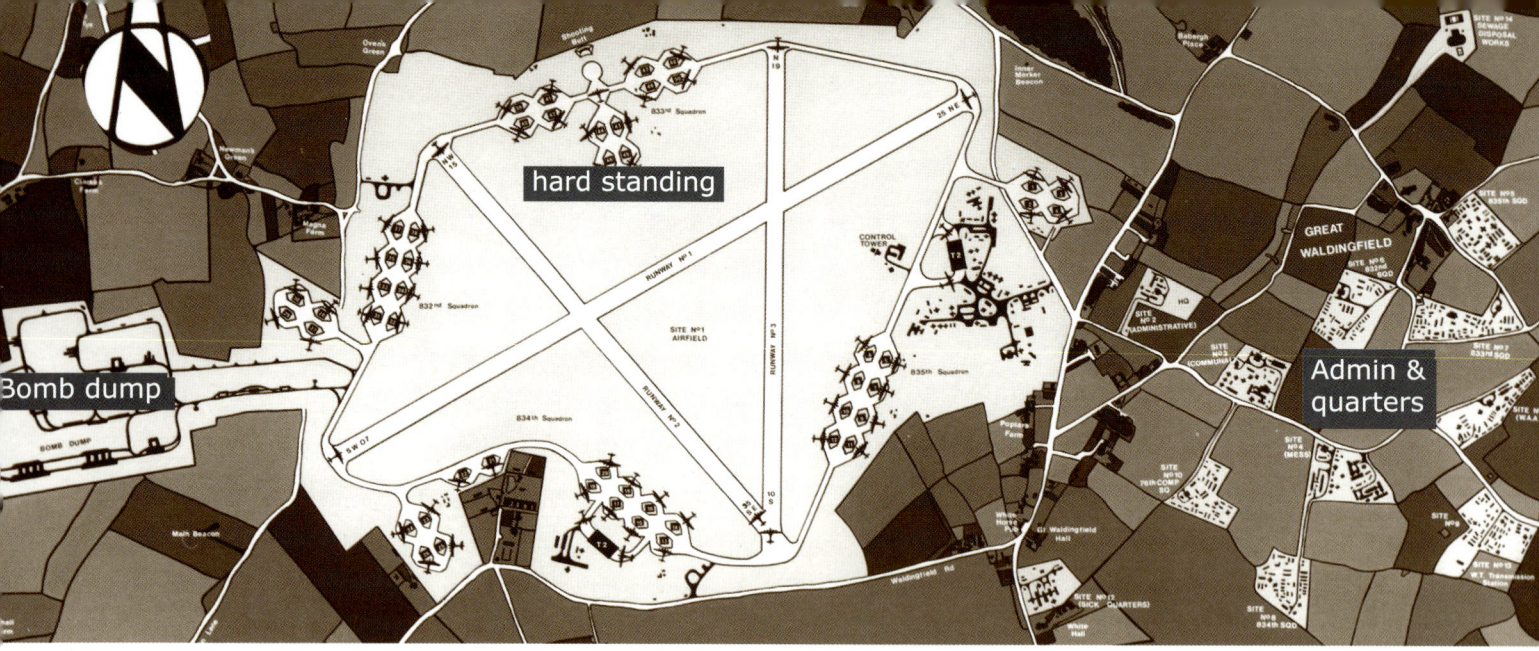

The children's war

Children seem to have experienced more excitement than fear in wartime Sudbury. 'It was such an exciting time,' is the comment you frequently heard from pensioners who were children then, though the story was obviously the reverse for those who lost fathers and brothers.

The war changed the town, the people and the quiet way of life. Beside the Americans, the town was full of soldiers as one regiment billeted in the town moved on and another took its place. There were bagpipes and military bands, small boys delighting in marching behind them on the Market Hill (and even among them). There were aircraft and searchlights to watch, pieces of shrapnel and other war debris to collect, and lots of uniformed men to watch and chat to, particularly after the generous Americans arrived with their giant bombers, gum and popcorn. Their small world also opened up with the influx of refugee children who had strange accents and big town ways. Playground arguments were common, but generally they got on together.

Children were drawn into the war effort as well, collecting salvage such as newspapers and books, picking fruit and gathering wild rose hips to be made into a syrup rich with vitamin D. The older children helped with harvesting and bottling fruit and vegetables for the winter.

I remember . . .

'We used to go to the Red House where the American officers were, and they would pass out cakes through the kitchen window. They made me a big chocolate cake when it came to my birthday. It was so big that it took three of us to carry it home. We had a party in Acton Square and everyone had some.'

Sylvia Byham - born 1929

I remember . . .

'I was allowed to post a letter just a few doors away from my home, and I saw this big man smiling down at me like some angel. He gave me a bag of popcorn and I took it home and gave it to my mother who didn't seem to approve. I don't remember exactly what happened next but I don't think I was allowed to eat it.'

Margaret Tracey, born 1941

above : Sudbury Airfield in 1944

Tragedy of young victims

There were risks involved in building an air base close to Sudbury as well as in a position where heavily-laden bombers would take off towards the town, but it was an acceptable risk in the urgency of wartime.

Fifteen-year-old Raymond Smith, was accustomed to the USAAF bombers going over the roof of his home. He was asleep in his bedroom at Woodhall Farm early on an autumn morning in 1944 when an engine failed on a B-17 Flying Fortress. Heavily-laden with bombs and fuel it failed to gain height on take off, veering off course and slicing through the roof of the former manor house. Raymond was rescued from the fire by his father but died the following day from extensive burns and shock. His father and the rest of the family, including his two sisters, survived unhurt.

The bomber ploughed on across farmland to explode half a mile from the end of the runway, the only survivor from the crew of nine being the pilot Clarence Hermann. He was blown clear in the explosion but suffered severe burns and brain damage, dying 32 years later. Woodhall was so badly damaged that it was demolished.

The bent and twisted propeller of the B-17 was dug out of the farmhouse moat in 1976, and is now part of a memorial to the 486th Bomb Group at the Eighth Air Force base at Barksdale in Louisiana.

Two months after the crash there was almost another tragedy in similar circumstances. On the last day of the year another B-17 lost an engine when it iced-up, caught fire and failed just as the heavily-laden bomber became airborne. But this time the pilot skimmed the town's roof tops then managed a crash landing alongside the crossing keeper's cottage at Little Cornard.

The crew of nine and the crossing keeper's family ran clear fearing an explosion, but the aircraft stayed intact and nobody was hurt.

above : Raymond Smith and Woodhall, before and after the crash
below : Remains of the B-17 bomber and the Barksdale Memorial.

The second death

The second tragic death of a child was in 1945 when a fuel tank from a USAAF Mustang fighter fell in stonemason Alfred Brett's garden in North Street and set fire to the house. Window cleaner Donald Malyon rescued three-year-old Terence Brett from the burning kitchen, but the child died of burns and shock although his mother recovered from her injuries. The coroner recorded a verdict of death by misadventure at the inquest, and praised the courage shown by Don Malyon who was slightly burned in the rescue.

above: The upper end of North Street where the fuel tank fell

The empty fuel tank should have been jettisoned over open ground, and the early release was blamed on the Mustang hitting an air pocket. The disposable tanks enabled the fighters to fly deeper into Germany as protective escort for bombers. Finding a jettisoned tank was the answer to a Sudbury schoolboy's prayer since they made an improvised canoe for use on the river.

Caring for the sick and injured

The pilot severely injured in the Woodhall Farm crash, was initially nursed at the base hospital at Acton Place which had a ward set aside for burns patients, the injury that every flyer dreaded and that was common when aircraft loaded with high-octane fuel crashed. Second Lieutenant Evangeline Blauvelt was 22 when she arrived at Acton in 1943 with a contingent of New England nurses assigned to set up 136 Station Hospital to deal with the sick and injured from a number of airfields including the 486th Station at Sudbury.

Once the Eighth Army Air Force began operations, sixty nurses worked 12-hour shifts caring for patients housed in temporary Nissen huts erected beside the 18th century Acton Place. Their patients ranged from dying flyers brought in from crashes to men with common infections. The medical staff included physicians, surgeons, a cardiac consultant and a dentist. Pot-bellied stoves were the only heating in the wards and at the age of 88, the former nurse remembered the severe winter of 1944/45 when the 486th aircraft were grounded by snow and ice for

above: Evangeline Blauvelt
below: Nurses at Acton place. Evangeline is sixth from the left.

many days. In January she helped to nurse a ward full of frost-bitten soldiers brought in from the Ardennes mountains after the German Army launched a major offensive in Belgium aimed at reaching the coast to cut the Allies' advance towards Germany. It was a costly struggle that history has named the Battle of the Bulge. The casualties were brought to Sudbury by train as they had been after the D-Day landings.

Lodging house for the Rising Sun (now Ivy Lodge) in Straw Lane

Off duty in Sudbury, Evangeline, or Vangie as she preferred to be called, met Mr and Mrs Bishop who kept the Rising Sun pub in Plough Lane. They welcomed her, and another nurse, to their home and fireside. For the young women so far from home, the Rising Sun, with its friendly lodging house and the occasional night's sleep on a feather bed, was near heaven. They ate well at the hospital but were well aware of their hosts' meagre rations. 'We took them any food we could get from our cooks who made us a cake to give to the Bishop's for their 25th wedding anniversary.'

It was the cold that ended Vangie's war. Before V E Day she was sent to a general hospital at Diss with pneumonia and finally returned to America on a hospital ship.

Vangie married - her surname became Hooker - and has a daughter. She retired to Sonora, California and keeps in touch with Sudbury wartime friends.

Love story that endures in print

One Anglo-American wartime romance is told in a book that captures the essence of Sudbury and Suffolk in those heady days. USAAF Staff Sergeant Robert Arbib simply calls her 'the Girl Joan' in *Here We Are Together - a notebook of an American Soldier in Britain*, a perceptive, sensitive view of wartime England that was a best seller. He came to Suffolk in 1942 with an engineering unit building airfields, and left England on D-day as an army war correspondent.

Joan Ramsey was his favourite girl in his 'favourite town' of Sudbury, working at the post office where he collected the mail for his unit which was building an airfield at Debach. 'A slender elfin blonde with a warm smile for everyone,' was how he described her in a chapter devoted to their courtship and way she, and Sudbury, brought him to a greater understanding of England.

He chose to spend much of his leisure

above : 'Here we are together' with cover illustration by Giles
Bob Arbib and Joan Ramsey during WWII

time in the town. There were jolly evenings in the pubs, nights he lodged at Gainsborough's House when it was a hotel and home-cooked meals in welcoming households including Joan's family home in Queens Road. He played chess with bank manager Vivian Goodman and went for long walks in the Suffolk countryside with Joan. He identified the birds and she taught him the names of wild flowers. His interest in ornithology played a major role in his later life.

Joan was pretty and bright, and at 19 ten years younger than the Yale-educated New Yorker who was already making a career in the advertising business on Madison Avenue. He wanted them to marry but she turned him down. 'He was older than me and I wasn't ready to settle down, I was having such a good time,' she explained, at the age of 85. They cooled the relationship and he wrote rather wistfully: 'She was too perfectly attuned to this Suffolk life to change . . . and it was too early to become tied to a future that was unknown, distant, alien and uncertain at best.'

The war over, he went back to the United States and a successful career in advertising, his accounts including Ford of America and Corona Typewriters. But away from the world of advertising he was a passionate ornithologist and conservationist. He wrote an award-winning book about the destruction of a wood on Long Island that had been his boyhood haunt, and others followed. Eventually he left Madison Avenue in his early 50s to become editor of the prestigious American Birds for the Audubon Society, and in that role he organised the first bird count on the continent.

He sent Joan a copy of *Here We Are Together* when it was published in 1946. Her reaction was a mixture of sadness and joy. 'It brought our days together flooding back,' she said. At about the same time she met her future husband - again across the counter in the Post Office. He was Roger Lynton, a naturalised German who had come to Sudbury as a refugee in the 1930s to work in the silk industry. He had fought with the British Army in Burma, changing his name to Lynton, the north Devon village close to where he had been stationed. Eventually he became managing director of Sudbury silk weavers Stephen Walters and Sons. Joan is now a widow.

Robert Arbib did marry an English woman. He came back after the war to wed Renee Johnson, the features editor of a national newspaper. He had met her at Elstree Studios while working as a dialogue advisor on a feature film about American servicemen in Britain. Both couples were friendly and exchanged visits after the war.

Bob Arbib died unexpectedly in 1987 after surgery at the age of 72. He took the title of his book from Winston Churchill's address to Congress in 1941 when he said: 'Here we are together defending all that to free men is dear.'

Bob Arbib and Joan Lynton, née Ramsey, in later life

Hush-hush Royal visits

King George VI visited Sudbury briefly on three occasions during the war. In 1944 the late Alan Phillips, who was liaison officer between Sudbury Council and the American base, was tipped off about the King's early morning arrival at the railway station and took along his five-year-old son Andrew. He recollects that he and his father, two policemen and the station staff were the only people around when the King came out of the station accompanied by General Bernard Montgomery, got into a staff car which sped off to Clare Priory which had been commandeered for D-Day planning. The General was in command of all the Allied ground forces on D-Day.

Local historian Barry Wall remembers the King arriving by train possibly in the same year. This arrival was also supposed to be a closely-guarded secret, but a crowd had gathered by the time his train pulled into the station, the news of the royal passenger having possibly leaked out as a result of the royal car being garaged overnight at the Black Boy pub. The King was grim-faced, refused to acknowledge the waves and cheers and demanded to know why the children in the crowd were not at school.

Gilman Game, then the teenage son of the manager of the Westminster Bank on Market Hill, recalls another occasion earlier in the war when a whisper went around the town that the King was arriving at the station on his way to inspect troops in the park at Melford Hall. 'Consequently small groups were waiting when three or four cars came up King Street with the King plainly visible in one as he acknowledged the scattered cheers. Later we heard a rumour that he was returning in the afternoon and I, and some other boys, perched on the footbridge at the end of the platform. The King said goodbye to various officers before boarding the train. The second he was through the door there was a hiss of steam and the train glided out of the station with various aides running alongside and climbing in as it moved.'

above : General Montgomery and George VI
left : Alan Phillips in the RAF

Sudbury drab and grey on a market day in the hard winter of 1944/45. Because of the shortage of film, few images survive of Sudbury in WWII. This photograph was taken by an American airman.

Killed in Burma

On the other side of the world the 14th Army of British and Commonwealth troops commanded by General William Slim had invaded Japanese occupied Burma from India at the beginning of the year. The force became known as 'the Forgotten Army' - the brutal jungle campaign being overshadowed by events in Europe. An early casualty was Sunday School teacher Private Leslie Everitt serving with the Queen's Own Royal West Kent Regiment. He was 24 and the son of grocer Albert Everitt and his wife Esther who also had an adjoining sweet shop in North Street, the family living above the shop. His parents gave Trinity United Reformed Church a font in his memory.

above : The font that the Everitts donated to the church in memory of their son

below : Leslie Everitt (inset) and his mother, Esther Everitt in her sweetshop in the early 50's

Leslie Everitt (inset) and his mother, Esther in her sweetshop in the early 1950's

The friends who died

Billy Hurst and Jimmy Pilgrim grew up together in Mill Lane, went to school together and both worked at Bakers Mill in Great Cornard. War separated them with Billy a corporal in the Queen's Own Royal West Kent Regiment, and Jimmy a Private in the 4th Suffolks. Both died less than a year apart. Billy was killed, aged 24, in June as the Germans fought a rear-guard action in northern Italy against the advancing Allies after Italy surrendered. His friend Jimmy had died as a Japanese prisoner of war in the Far East.

Billy and Jimmy - boyhood chums

The Rector's son

As Rector of St Gregory's Church in Sudbury, Canon John Hughes conducted the funerals of servicemen brought back to Sudbury for burial, but not that of his youngest son. Flying Officer John Douglas Hughes was buried in a cemetery at Hanover in northern Germany, killed flying as navigator on a Mosquito light bomber of 627 Squadron that carried out low level bombing and target marking from its base in Cambridgeshire. He was 23 when his aircraft was reported missing, and had already flown many sorties over Germany. His father was Rector of Sudbury and mayor's chaplain from 1929 until 1957, and lived at the then rectory in Gainsborough Street.

The Rectory in Gainsborough Street

Losses in the air continued during 1944. Flying Officer John Marshall's Lancaster failed to return from an attack on Rheydt in the Rhineland in September. The Red Cross discovered that his aircraft had crashed and three survivors had been taken prisoner. The 23-year-old former Sudbury police constable was not among them. His grave is in a cemetery in the Reichswald Forest where airmen's bodies from various isolated sites were reburied after the war. One of the great RAF heroes of WWII was killed in the same raid. Wing Commander Guy Gibson, of Dambuster fame, acted as master bomber, his aircraft crashing in flames in Holland. He had won the Victoria Cross for his part in the 'bouncing bomb' raid on the Mohne, Eder and Sorpe dams in 1943.

They flew by moonlight

A report 'missing in action' was agonising for families who lived in hope, sometimes for years, that the missing man was a prisoner of war, or lying unidentified in a hospital.

Such was the trauma for the Sudbury parents of Flying Officer (Arnold) Keith Dean whose aircraft crashed on a secret mission.

Their son flew with the highly secret 161 Squadron which took off on moonlit nights from a heavily camouflaged airstrip in Bedfordshire to drop Special Operations Executive (SOE) agents, together with arms and equipment, into occupied Europe where they organised and supported resistance groups. The Squadron also collected those who survived, and RAF crew found and sheltered by resistance workers.

Keith Dean loved flying, belonged to Sudbury's Air Training Corps. and enlisted in the RAF as soon as he was 18. He trained as air crew in Canada and his skills as a bomb aimer were crucial on these missions to drop people and equipment on target.

But low level flying over occupied Europe was a risky business and in August his Halifax was shot down in Holland with three Dutch agents on board. His parents living at The Chantry in Stour Street knew only that their 20-year-old son was missing, presumed killed. They finally learned details of the crash when the pilot was liberated from a prison camp at the end of the war. Accountant Ernest Dean refused to accept that his son was dead and advertised for information in Holland. This led to finding a grave marked 'F/O Dean' tended by villagers in Engelen in southern Holland. After a long fight Ernest Dean won the right to have the body exhumed, but the height and teeth of the skeleton did not appear to match his son's medical records. Ernest Dean died still nursing the hope that his son had survived the crash. It was not until 1989 that Keith's sister Pamela had his name added on an individual plate to those on already on the War Memorial.

The impact of D-Day

D-Day, 6 June, 1944, is remembered for Operation Overlord, the largest-ever combined amphibious and airborne landing in history when more than 156,000 Allied troops landed in Normandy. In the following days and weeks huge numbers of support troops and vehicles joined them, and Sudbury saw part of their great trek southwards to the Channel ports on the way to France.

On D-Day some of the first contingents of these reinforcements passed through the town from early morning, forming an erratically moving queue travelling southward through the town centre, up Ballingdon Hill and onwards to Halstead. It rumbled on as a seemingly endless stream of tanks, troop carriers, petrol bowsers, bren gun carriers and other paraphernalia of war.

As an eleven-year-old schoolboy Peter Minter, later the managing director of the Bulmer Brick and Tile Company, watched it from a window at Salters Hall School. 'It was an incredible sight. The noise was terrific and the buildings shook. In Gainsborough Street Sherman tanks cut notches in the granite kerbstones. We were waving and cheering and the troops waved back. There was a huge buzz of excitement in the air, we felt we must win the war now.'

The D-Day experience

Private Freddie Pepper was a keen member of the Stour Boat Club but that was no preparation for a rough crossing of the English Channel to land on D-Day with a battalion of the Durham Light Infantry. He, and about 150 others, had already spent four days in port in cramped conditions aboard an American Navy landing craft. They scrambled ashore on Gold Beach, one survivor later wrote: 'after 200 to 300 yards all hell broke loose as shellfire flew around.'

Freddie Pepper survived the landing, and the action as the Allies fought their way across France, only to die of wounds in Belgium three months later. He was the only surviving child of Frederick Pepper, chief clerk at Sudbury goods yard, and his wife Maud. Sudbury remembered him as a smart young man who worked at the Post Office and took part in their concert party variety shows. He was also keen on sport and a one-time secretary of the Boat Club.

Sudbury lost surprisingly few men in the aftermath of the D-Day landings. The first was Lance Corporal Douglas Stock serving in the Irish Guards, who died in the battle to secure Cagny, a small town near Caen.

top left : British troops assembling on Red Beach on D-Day, with men of 1st Suffolks in the background

left : Lance Corporal Stock

right : Disembarkation at the Normandy Landings

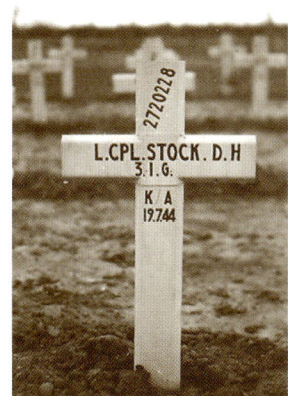

It was part of the Allies' struggle to break out of the established Normandy beachhead against fierce opposition. The tanks of the Guards Armoured Division fought it out field by field with German Panzers and succeeded in taking the town. Douglas Stock was killed by a mortar shell the following day. The 24-year-old was a reporter on the Suffolk Free Press when he was conscripted in 1940, and was married. Little is known about the death of RAF Sergeant Harold Mills apart from a report in the Suffolk Free Press that he 'was missing, believed killed, in an accident in France.' He died in August 1944, a month in which the Allies were fighting to break out of Normandy to the south. He was a twin, and married to the former Ethel Collar from Bures. His parents lived in Melford Road.

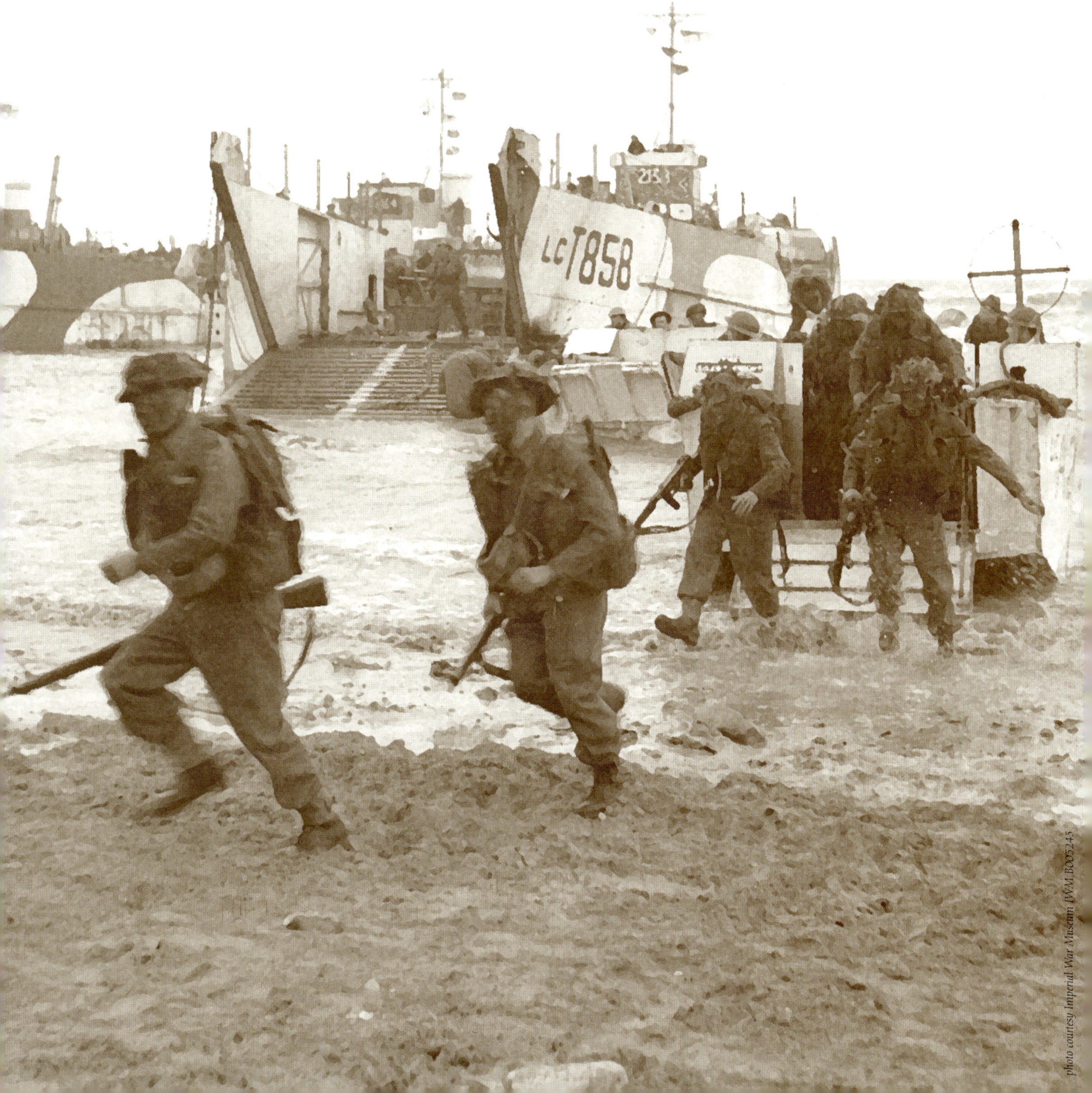

photo courtesy Imperial War Museum IWM B005245

Victory in sight and cruelty uncovered

Peace at last

Victory in Europe Day - 8th May, 1945, lives bright in the memory of those who experienced the outpouring of joy and relief that Europe was finally at peace after more than five years of struggle, pain and grief.

Sudbury celebrated all day and long into the night. Flags and bunting were brought out of storage to decorate shops, offices and homes. The Union Jack, the Stars and Stripes and flags of other Allied nations fluttered above the Town Hall. At dusk windows that had been blacked out for all the war years were thrown open so that light streamed out.

It seemed as if most of the population of Sudbury was on the Market Hill where loudspeakers relayed dance music in the afternoon and evening, and at one point the bells of all the three medieval churches rang triumphant peals. Mayor Sydney Wheeler, who had held the reins all through the war, spoke from the steps of the Town Hall, and St Peter's Church was packed for a hastily-arranged service of thanksgiving for peace.

At dusk the Market Hill was lit by searchlights trained on the Church and the crowd became ever more boisterous with a soldier sitting on the shoulders of Gainsborough's bronze statue.

I remember . . .

'On VE Day my little gang went around the town making a cacophonous noise with a makeshift band. I had a biscuit tin on a piece of string around my neck and two pieces of wood as drumsticks. Everyone was in good humour and tolerant towards little boys' outlandish behaviour.'

Andrew Phillips, born 1939, son of town clerk Alan Phillips

There is a story that a paratrooper took a woman's garment from a washing line in the Acton Square area, put it on over his uniform, and was chased to the Market Hill by the furious owner.

A bonfire built by local Boy Scouts lit the night sky on the Croft, and the crowd on the Market Hill danced and sang the favourite wartime songs. The celebrations went on so late that finally the Mayor asked the revellers to go home so that people living on the Hill could get some sleep.

There was a reminder during the day that another fight had yet to be won. It came in Winston Churchill's victory broadcast that was relayed to the crowd. 'Advance Britannia - long live the cause of freedom,' the Prime Minister told the nation. 'We may allow ourselves a brief period of rejoicing; but let us not forget for a moment the toil and efforts that lie ahead. Japan with all her treachery and greed remains unsubdued.' It would be three months and two atom bombs later before the Japanese surrendered.

left : The King's letter of thanks to a member of Sudbury Home Guard

1945

'The Market Hill was lit up by two searchlights, one near the library and the other close to Burkitts Lane. They were trained on the spire of St Peter's and they lit up the market place. There were so many people that you couldn't move. I remember having a job to push through the crowd. The pubs were all open and people were singing and dancing, everyone was so happy.'

Memory of VE Day celebrations
Peter B Smith, born 1935

The terrible aftermath to Singapore

It would be another four months before the world learned the truth of what had befallen the 100,000 British and Commonwealth servicemen taken prisoner at Singapore in February 1942. Little had been heard of their fate and the Japanese had refused the International Red Cross access to the prison camps. After Japan surrendered in September 1945, prisoners who were more corpse than alive and almost naked were found in their prison camps. Among survivors from the 4th and 5th Suffolks were men from Sudbury and the surrounding villages.

Pre-printed postcards provided by their captors had assured families that they were well. The truth was very different. The Japanese had starved their prisoners while forcing them, under the constant threat of beatings, at heavy manual work in the unremittingly hostile tropical climate.

Even in the monsoon season they had worked twelve hours a day while debilitated by disease and suffering from tropical ulcers that ate into limbs and eyes. One in three prisoners died of cholera, malnutrition, tuberculosis, beri-beri, exhaustion, or from beatings and summary execution. They were not slaves in the absolute sense because the Japanese paid men in the ranks the equivalent of a penny a day with which they bought fruit from passing traders to aid their meagre diet.

The 5th Suffolks were part of the huge work force that built the notorious 'Death Railway' stretching 260 miles across Thailand into Burma, including the bridge over the River Kwai immortalised in the 1957 film. At least 13,000 Allied prisoners of war died building the railway and many others met their deaths slaving in docks, mines and on construction work elsewhere in the new Japanese empire. The two Suffolk battalions lost more than 760 of those who landed at Singapore - nearly three quarters of them dying in captivity, including at least 12 from Sudbury.

Images of the liberated survivors shocked the world, many men weighed less than six stones after years on a starvation diet of as little as a cup of rice a day, supplemented by a few vegetables. Their home-coming was delayed for months in order to treat their medical problems and restore their emaciated bodies to something like normality. Many did not come home. Former Suffolk Free Press reporter Lance Corporal Albert Bear of the 5th Suffolks died just a week after the world celebrated Victory over Japan Day (V-J Day), having survived the deprivations for so long. It was an extra sorrow for Walter and Jane Bear to lose their 24-year-old son when he was so close to survival.

Cholera had killed 25-year-old Private Philip Cahill, of the 5th Suffolks who also helped to build the railway. He died in an epidemic that killed 214 in one camp alone in 1943. A survivor recorded that 32 died in one night, their bodies piled up 'like so much firewood'. Philip had worked at Sudbury Mill before the war and lived with his family in Cross Street. Private Thomas Codling of the 1st Cambridgeshire Regiment died on the same day, aged 29, and could have been another victim of the cholera epidemic. His wife living in East Street with their child, had waited more than a year for news of him before a postcard arrived to say that he was safe and well. In fact he was already dead.

A month later Private Alexander Bowles of the 4th Suffolks had died at the age of 25, despite previously being so strong and athletic that he had won trophies racing with the Essex Cycle Club. His widowed mother Rose, living in Sandy Lane, had been optimistic because she had received a postcard reporting he was fit and well. Private George Cecil was one of five more Sudbury men who died in the next few months as malnutrition and disease killed an increasing number of those toiling on the railway. He was already dead from cerebral malaria when a postcard reached his parents Thomas and Mary Cecil telling them he was well and a prisoner. At 22, he was the youngest of their five sons serving in the Army.

Ten days later Private Robert 'Joe' Sargeant died from beri-beri, a disease caused by vitamin deficiency; the body wastes away but the limbs swell, and death often results from heart failure. He was 27 and had married his sweetheart Doris just before being shipped out to the Far East. Private James 'Jimmy' Pilgrim serving with the 4th Suffolks was another who died working on the railway at

this time. He was 25, and had lived with his mother in Mill Lane.

The toll continued with the death of Company Quartermaster Sergeant Robert McAusland McIntyre, 33, of the 5th Suffolks, a skilled textile designer in Sudbury's weaving industry who lived with his wife Cecilia in Cornard Road. He died from diarrhoea and exhaustion. One of three brothers, Lance Corporal Robert 'Jimmy' Moore, 26, of the 4th Suffolks was another of the many married men who succumbed. His wife Amy worked at the County Cinema and his older brother Joseph had been lost during 1941 in the sinking of *HMS Chakdina*.

Death Railway builder Private Billy Nunn, 24, of the 5th Suffolks, was killed just before the end of the war when the Americans bombed the island of Formosa where he had been shipped for forced labour. The pre-war apprentice carpenter was the son of a WWI veteran and member of a Church Street family. His mother had his Suffolk Regiment cap badge dipped in silver, and wore it until her death when it was buried with her.

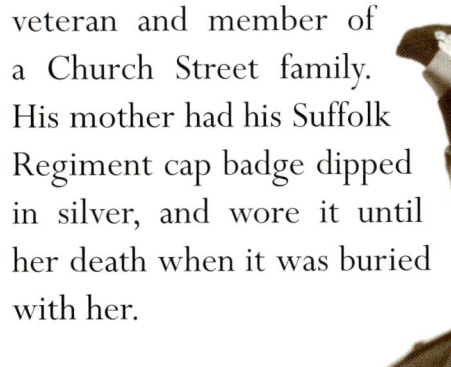

opposite : Grave of Albert Bear in Thailand
above : Robert Sargeant at his own wedding
above : The two Moore brothers (Joseph, left -'Jimmy', right)
right : Private Billy Nunn

Postcard from hell

This wartime postcard from Thailand hides the suffering of one of many thousands who spent much of WWII as prisoners of the Japanese. Sent by Cecil Wells, a young Captain in the 5th Suffolk Regiment, to his mother in Friars Street, it gives no clue to the prisoners' terrible sufferings at the hands of their captors. Two of these postcards were the only news that reached her during the three and a half years he was in captivity. He was 21 and had just completed a law degree at Cambridge when he sailed for Singapore with the regiment, surviving both a wound in the battle for the island and then long captivity. After the war he joined a local firm of solicitors and retired as senior partner of Bates, Wells and Braithwaite. He died in the year 2000 aged 82.

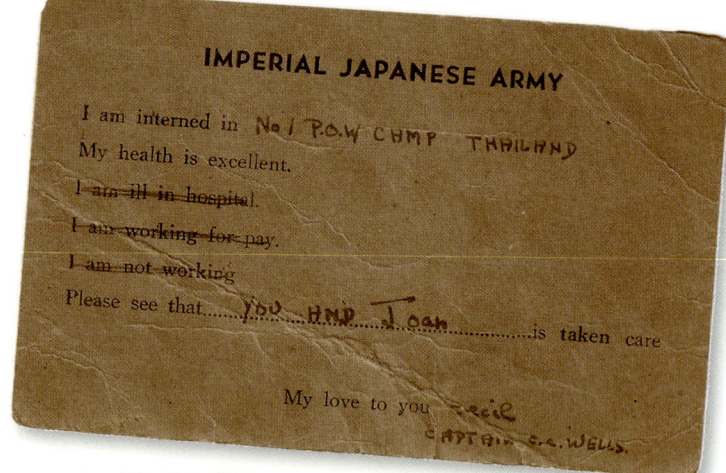

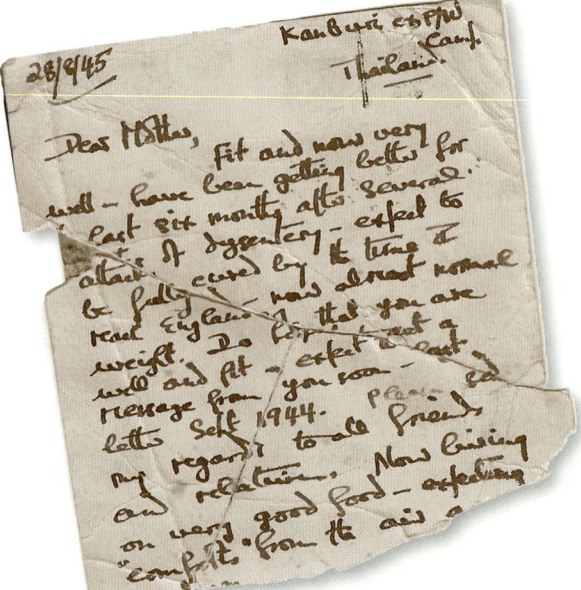

above top : wartime postcard
above middle : sketch of the Captain by a fellow POW
below right : Cecil Wells in 1939
top left Cecil Wells' first letter home
left : sketch of prisoners' hut

This worn photograph belonged to Ted Bacon, one of Sudbury's 5th Suffolk survivors. It seems to have been set up by the Japanese for propaganda purposes. The clues are the ill-fitting uniforms and the men's bony wrists and unsmiling faces. On the back Ted Bacon wrote: '5th Suffolk Regiment: total deaths to date 325 men of whom 22 killed in action. Rest of the dead died through tropical diseases in Thailand during building of Burma-Thai Railway.'

Unravelling a puzzle

Just before the fall of Singapore Gunner George Seal sent a telegram to his mother assuring her he was well and safe and not to worry. It ended 'with fondest love and kisses,' It would not reach Susan Seal at her home in Ballingdon Street until August 1944, two years after she was told her son was missing presumed killed. He was eventually recorded as having died at sea two weeks after the island fell to the Japanese. It is possible that 22-year-old George Seal managed to board one of the many boats that sailed from the chaos of Singapore harbour as the Japanese closed in, many of them only to be bombed and sunk by the enemy. News of his death was a double tragedy for his parents Susan and Arthur Seal. In 1943 their younger son, Reginald, also a gunner in the Royal Artillery, had been fatally injured in an explosion while sea bathing with comrades, dying of multiple injuries in Clacton Hospital at the age of 20. East Coast beaches were heavily mined and it is possible that he stepped on one.

The brutality of the Japanese army towards prisoners had its roots in their warrior culture tradition that a soldier must kill himself rather than face dishonour by surrendering. In their view prisoners were lesser beings, and they meted out even worse treatment to the natives of the countries they occupied in South East Asia. The pre-printed postcards provided for prisoners to send home and the payment of a penny a day were token acknowledgments of international agreement on the treatment of prisoners of war. Prisoners knew that if they wrote the facts their postcard would be destroyed.

Death on a Hell Ship

In the late summer of 1944 the Japanese had shipped the fittest survivors from the railway construction to work as forced labour in Japan and other parts of their empire, cramming, them into cargo holds for long voyages. The men suffered, and many died, in hot, unsanitary, airless conditions with little food or water. Allied submarines targeted the unmarked vessels unaware of their human cargoes. Two Sudbury men were among 400 who died when the submarine *USS Pampanito* torpedoed the *Kachidoki Maru*, a former American cargo ship that had been captured by the Japanese. The dead included former regular soldier Private Sidney Mumford, who had been a bricklayer and lived in Church Street with his wife Eva and their son. The outbreak of the war had put him back into uniform at the age of 35. He died together with Private Ephraim Cole, aged 28, whose family lived in Garden Place off Cross Street. Both men served in the 5th Battalion, Bedfordshire and Hertfordshire Regiment.

Eva Mumford, like so many others, had received only scant information about what was happening to her husband during his long imprisonment. Initially she was told he was missing, the next year a postcard from a prison camp gave the news that he was 'fit and well.' It was not until the Spring of 1945 that she was told he was again 'missing,' and finally after the peace she learned he had been dead for more than a year. The submarine *USS Pampanito* has a new life at the San Francisco Maritime National Park.

above : The passenger liner SS President Harrison that later became hellship, Kachidoki Maru
right : Submarine USS Pampanito
far right : Far East war veteran, Harold Lock in 2009

Achieving compensation

More than half a century after the war a Sudbury man's testimony of his treatment as a prisoner played a significant role in the British Government's decision to pay compensation to survivors. In March 2000, former BBC war correspondent Martin Bell, then MP for Tatton, who served in the 5th Suffolks, quoted to a hushed House of Commons from the vivid memories of former Sudbury publican Harold Lock who had been captured in Java in 1942. As a 17-year-old boy sailor he had swum ashore after *HMS Jupiter* hit a mine, and spent the greater part of the war building an airfield on a tropical island in preparation for Japan's planned invasion of Australia.

Of life on the island he said: 'Death had become commonplace and we were getting like robots, all feelings disappearing except the desire to cling to life. It is strange how precious everything seems when you are on the verge of death as most of us were. For three and a half years most of those who survived faced the prospect of death at all times. Those who could not work died. Those who could, worked on in a vermin-ridden rage. All of them, I believe, were marked for life.'

The Labour Government spokesman's response to Martin Bell's intervention was to reiterate its position that Far East prisoners of war could not be singled out for special treatment. But the ex-prisoners campaign gained momentum. Nine months later the British Government capitulated, agreeing to pay £10,000 to each survivor and to the widows of those who had died. The victory was hugely satisfying for Harold, who in 1995 had broken his long silence to write about his experiences and see it published as The Forgotten Men. 'I'd had surgery for cancer and I realised I ought to write down what had happened to me while I could so that people knew the truth of what went on.'

The slim book sold well and led to him forming the South Suffolk Far East Prisoners of War Association, as well as a strong bond with former Beirut hostage Terry Waite. This resulted in a series of Sudbury reunions that attracted former Far East prisoners from a wide area. In 2005 the two travelled to the Far East together to visit Java and Singapore, a trip that gave Harold a degree of closure.

Legacy of the camps

Tall and broad shouldered he had weighed only six stone when the war ended, less than half his normal weight. Some of his fellow prisoners were in a worse condition, and men continued to die even after a Royal Navy contingent arrived at their camp bringing food and medical care. Many were suffering from beri-beri with swollen limbs resulting from vitamin deficiency in their diet which consisted mainly of white rice. The health problems that lingered after repatriation included TB, potentially fatal parasitic diseases, and reccurring bouts of malaria.

Eventually there was substantial physical healing but Harold Lock asserted that none of the men he knew after the war - and there were about 40 survivors in the Sudbury area - was ever the same again. Psychological damage was profound, with ex-prisoners experiencing nightmares and flashbacks that tended to become worse with age. Former prisoners often kept their experiences to themselves, partly out of fear of being disbelieved and partly to block out persistant and painful memories.

Harold exorcised many of his demons when he first came home, with a three-month-long drinking binge financed from back pay. His companions were fellow POWs Ernie Raimo and Len Brett who also lived in Cross Street. 'We got drunk every day, we just wanted to forget. We only came home on Fridays to change our clothes. We slept in churchyards, wherever, some nights it was in police cells but they left the doors open, gave us tea in the morning and sent us on our way. People were good to us.'

When the money ran out he went back to the Navy for a short while but was discharged suffering from depression, eventually becoming landlord of the Plough in Melford Road. His physical legacies of imprisonment were a double hernia caused by carrying excessively heavy loads, a scar on his ankle where a bayonet jab went gangrenous, and being unable to father a child, attributed to extreme deprivation at a young age. At 85, the last Sudbury survivor of the Far East prisoners of war had neither forgotten nor forgiven: 'In my opinion a people that can do such things could do it again.'

Harold Lock as a boy sailor

Accidents and disease

Death in wartime came in other guises apart from being killed or fatally wounded in action. Excluding those who died as prisoners of the Japanese, illness and accident accounted for at least ten deaths listed on the war memorial. Some might have occurred naturally in civilian life but others died because of the conditions and situations in which they served.

The death toll continued after the peace. Leading Aircraftman Robert Pettit took part in the Burma campaign in which the RAF had sustained General Slim's Army as it fought the Japanese in the jungle. He survived the war much to the joy of his parents. His father, also Robert, was well known in Sudbury as he had combined his normal workload as managing clerk of a legal practice with the role of town clerk while Alan Phillips served in the RAF. He also chaired the Sudbury Wings for Victory savings campaign, and was at one time the town's billeting officer. Robert Pettit and his wife Florence expected their 23-year-old only son to be home in Priory Road at the beginning of 1946, but he died from an illness in Rangoon just before Christmas.

Meanwhile back in Europe, polio was blamed for the death in August 1945 of Gunner Hubert Bayfield, a Territorial soldier who had survived the evacuation from Dunkirk and action with the Eighth Army in North Africa, Italy, France and Germany. He was buried in a war cemetery in Austria. His parents lived in Priory Walk.

1946
A long struggle begins to win the peace

With war over in both Europe and the Far East, it soon became obvious to Britain's war-weary population that austerity and self sacrifice were not at an end. In Sudbury, as elsewhere, there were still food queues, demobbed servicemen still continued to wear their uniforms as working clothes and 'make do and mend' was still essential because of the shortage of raw materials and manufactured goods. A Black Market flourished, a stall holder in Sudbury Market being fined for selling an electric razor above the set retail price. There was also a desperate shortage of housing which led to Sudbury Council building houses in Cats Lane.

Housewives continued to wrestle with the restrictions of food rationing including a cut in the weekly allowance of butter, margarine and cooking fat. Then in May - a year on from peace in Europe - bread was rationed for the first time. In mid-summer the Government warned there would be insufficient coal for the winter, a chilling thought as most homes relied on a coal fire for heating. Power cuts followed in that winter for both industrial and domestic users and the Town Council turned off all but three of the town's 156 streetlights.

Hundreds of Sudbury workers lost their jobs where employers relied on power from the national grid, and households had to cope without electricity in the mornings and evenings. This would be the cruellest cut of all because the winter of 1946/47 proved to be one of the most severe recorded, with snow and heavy frosts from January to mid-March. Snowdrifts up to six feet deep blocked roads cutting off many communities outside the town for days on end.

When the thaw came it was followed by gales and the worst floods in the Stour Valley in living memory. Flood water was reported to be three feet deep in Ballingdon Street, and around All Saints Church people took refuge in their bedrooms. A fund was launched locally to help those in need.

The way of life in Britain gradually improved and there were major reforms in education and with the launch of the National Health Service, but it would be 1957 before Prime Minister Harold Macmillan felt confident in telling a rally: 'Most of our people have never had it so good.'

I remember . . .

'An enduring memory of my wartime childhood was a yearning for bananas. The nearest I, or any other child, got to one was a cut-out illustration of a hand of bananas stuck to glass door of Lefley's, the greengrocer and fruiterer in North Street. At the end of the war a banana was brought to my school in North Street by a child whose father had come back from abroad. It was a small black and yellow thing on cotton wool in a shoe box, as though ready for burial. After being displayed at assembly it was auctioned for a penny a ticket. I didn't win it, but for me it was a symbol that the war was ended and that things would get better - and, by and large, they did.'

Reverend Tony Moore, born 1934

Priscilla, a woman's war

All the names of those who died 'for King and Country' on Sudbury War Memorial are of men who lost their lives serving in the two World Wars, but among the Commonwealth War Graves Commission headstones in Sudbury cemetery is that of a young woman who went to school in Sudbury. She was Lance Corporal Priscilla Carter who died aged 20, in a road accident while serving with the Auxilliary Territorial Service. Her name was never submitted for inclusion on the town memorial perhaps because her parents, oil engineer Edwin Carter and his wife Mabel, had moved away to West Essex long before she was killed in August 1946, although they chose to have her buried in the town cemetery. The inscription reads; 'In loving memory of our darling Priscilla - Mother Father Helen and Margie.' An inquest into Priscilla's death heard that she died from head injuries after the military vehicle she was driving overturned close to the Hampshire/Surrey border.

'She was bright and always a bit of tomboy' remembered Mrs Heather Bell who was her friend at Mill Lane School. 'We used to walk on the Water Meadows and she would come to our home in Cross Street, she lived in Friars Street and had two sisters.'

Priscilla died in peacetime but she was eligible for commemoration by the Commonwealth War Graves Commission because she was still in uniform and died within the 1947 cut off point. Her headstone is one of a group erected by the Commission in a corner of the cemetery. Flowers appear on her grave from time to time - someone else remembers her.

right : Priscilla served in the Auxiliary Territorial Service, (the Queen also served in the ATS when she was Princess Elizabeth)

below : Trio of WWII headstones - Priscilla's in the foreground

The men that Sudbury remembers

1914-1918

Abbott Private Frederick Robert, Manchester Regiment (36) d.26/3/18 *No known grave, Arras Memorial, France*

Adams Pte Frederick Charles, The Queen's (Royal West Surrey Regt) (21) d.21/12/18 *b. Mikra British Cemetery, Kalamaria, Greece* — 70

Ager, Pte Stanley Phillip, Middlesex Regiment (23) d.8/10/16 *No known grave, Thiepval Memorial, Somme, France*

Albon Pte Ernest Frank, Suffolk Regiment d.30/8/18 *b.Ecoust-St. Mein British Cemetery, France* — 51

Albon Pte Frederick John, Suffolk Regiment d.12/10/16 *No known grave, Thiepval Memorial, Somme* — 51

Allen Sergeant Joseph Edward, Suffolk Regiment (30) d.18/2/15 *No known grave, Menin Gate, Ypres, Belgium*

Ambrose Pte Walter E, Queen's Own (Royal West Kent Regt) (24) d. 7/10/16 *b.Warlencourt British Cemetery, France*

Ames Rifleman Ernest Cecil (served as Johnson), London Regiment (28) d.29/9/18 *b.Kandahar Farm Cemetery, Belgium*

Argent Pte Harry James, East Lancashire Regiment (31) d.3/11/14 *No known grave, Ploegsteert Memorial, Belgium* — 5

Armes Captain Raymond Linay, North Staffordshire Regiment (37) d.9/4/16. *No known grave, Basra Memorial, Iraq* — 32

Armes TD Lieut. Colonel William Morriss, Suffolk Regiment (43) d.12/8/15 *No known grave, Helles Memorial, Turkey* — 19

Barber Pte Frederick Harry, Suffolk Regiment (20) d.18/12/14 *b.Sudbury Cemetery, Suffolk* — 16

Barber Pte Harry, Suffolk Regiment d.11/3/16 *b.Le Touquet-Paris Plage Communal Cemetery, France* — 44

Bareham Driver Albert Daniel, Royal Field Artillery d.26/8/18 *b.Taranto Town Cemetery Extension, Italy*

Bareham Pte Bertie, Suffolk Regiment d.18/8/16 *No known grave, Thiepval Memorial, Somme*

Baring Pte Charles Alexander, Australian Imperial Force (23) d.4/9/16 *No known grave, Villers-Bretonneux Memorial, Somme* — 45

Baring Second Lieut. Cecil Christopher, Queen's Own (Royal W Kent Regt) (20) d. 21/3/18 *b.Roye New British Cemetery, Somme* — 45

Baring Lance Corporal Ernest, Australian Imperial Force (27) d.2/4/17 *b.Vaulx Hill Cemetery, France* — 45

Baring Second Lieut. Reginald Arthur, Royal Air Force (19) d.9/6/18 *No known grave, Arras Flying Services Memorial, France* — 45

Barrell Pte Charles A, Grenadier Guards (32) d.1/3/19 *b.St. Andrew's Churchyard, Bulmer, Essex* — 70

Basham Rifleman Herbert William, The King's (Liverpool Regt) (29) d. 20/9/17 *No known grave, Tyne Cot Memorial, near Ypres* — 56

Bayes Private Charles John, London Regiment (33) d.10/8/16 *b.Hebuterne Military Cemetery, Somme* — 44

Bear Air Mechanic 2nd Class Edward Marshall, Royal Air Force (34) d.8/3/19 *b.Sudbury Cemetery*

Beer Sapper Frederick Arthur, Royal Engineers (21) d.14/9/15 *b.Alexandria (Chatby) Military Cemetery, Egypt* — 23

Beevis Pte Percy, Loyal North Lancashire Regiment (26) d.14/7/16 *No known grave, Thiepval Memorial, Somme*

Bell Pte Albert James, Suffolk Regiment d. 8/11/18 *b.St. Sever Cemetery Extension, Rouen, France*

Bell Pte Clarence William James, York and Lancaster Regiment (21) d.23/10/14 *No known grave, Ploegsteert Memorial, Belgium*

Belsham Able Seaman Edwin, Royal Navy *unable to trace record at present time*

Belsham Able Seaman Henry John, Royal Navy (19) d.17/6/16 *No known grave, Chatham Naval Memorial, Kent* — 53

Binks Pte Sidney, Suffolk Regiment d.5/5/15 *No known grave, Menin Gate Memorial, Ypres* — 12

Blythe Rifleman Edward Sydney, Rifle Brigade (22) d.2/12/17 *No known grave, Tyne Cot Memorial, near Ypres* — 61

Blythe Corporal Maurice Hammond, Royal Engineers d.1/11/18 *b.Awoingt British Cemetery, France* — 70

Bond Rifleman Harold, London Regiment d.1/7/16 *No known grave, Thiepval Memorial, Somme* — 40

Botham Corporal Arthur Walford, Suffolk Regiment d.3/7/16 *No known grave, Thiepval Memorial, Somme*

Braybrook Gunner William, Machine Gun Corps (26) d.21/3/18 *No known grave, Arras Memorial, France*

Bridgman Gunner Frank, Royal Garrison Artillery (29) d.15/2/16 *b.Kut War Cemetery, Iraq* — 33

Bristow Corporal Robert Charles, Lincolnshire Regiment (33) d.5/9/18 *b.Lebucquiere Communal Cemetery, France*

Brown Pte William Henry, Suffolk Regiment (25) d.20/4/15 *b.Bedford House Cemetery, Ypres* — 12

Buckle Pte Sidney James, Essex Regiment d.20/10/16 *No known grave, Thiepval Memorial, Somme*

Bunn Pte William, Suffolk Regiment (19) d.2/11/17 *b.Gaza War Cemetery, Israel* — 60

Byford Rifleman Albert, Sherwood Foresters (Notts and Derby Regt) d.21/11/17 *b.Lijssenthoek Military Cemetery, Belgium*

Byham Pte Albert Robert, Suffolk Regiment (27) d.6/9/15 *b.7th Field Ambulance Cemetery, Turkey*

Byham Driver Leonard Charles, Royal Field Artillery (23) d.25/9/17 *b.Canada Farm Cemetery, Ypres* — 34

Cansdale Pte John Thomas, East Surrey Regiment (30) d.5/8/17 *No known grave, Menin Gate Memorial, Ypres* — 56

Cardy Corporal Maurice Walter, Royal Fusiliers (26) d.6/8/15 *b.Cité Bonjean Military Cemetery, Armentieres, France* — 27

Cardy Pte Robert Carl, Royal Fusiliers d.5/8/15 *b.Cité Bonjean Military Cemetery, Armentieres, France* — 27

Carter Pte William Charles, Australian Imperial Force *date and place of death not known* — 26

Cattling Pte Herbert, King's Liverpool Regiment *unable to trace record at present time*

Chaplin Pte Francis Harry, Royal Fusiliers (19) d.30/11/17 *No known grave, Cambrai Memorial, Louverval, France*

Chinery Pte George Frederick, Royal Warwickshire Regiment (22) d.4/5/17 *No known grave, Arras Memorial, France*

Chinery Rifleman James, West Yorkshire Regiment d.16/4/18 *No known grave, Tyne Cot Memorial, near Ypres*

Clark Pte Arthur Claude, South Staffordshire Regiment (19) d.26/10/17 *No known grave, Tyne Cot Memorial, near Ypres* — 56

Clark Pte Arthur Leonard, Essex Regiment, (25) d.18/10/15 *b.Wimereux Communal Cemetery, France*

Clark Pte Harry William, Royal Berkshire Regiment (22) d.27/8/16 *b.Karasouli Military Cemetery, Greece* — 56

Clarke Lance Corporal Walter Mark, Suffolk Regiment (39) d.9/4/17 *b.Tilloy British Cemetery, France*

Clover Lieut. Harwood Linay, Royal Flying Corps & Royal Dublin Fus. (23) d.23/12/16 *b.Sudbury Cemetery* — 48

Coates Pte Edwin Harry, Middlesex Regiment d.14/3/15 *No known grave, Le Touret Memorial, France*

Cook Pte Walter March, Middlesex Regiment (33) d.10/11/18 *b.Maubeuge-Centre Cemetery, France* — 64

Coote Pte John, Northamptonshire Regiment (39) d.4/5/17 *b.Savona Town Cemetery, Italy* — 53

Couch, Pte Herbert William, Suffolk Regiment (24) d.11/7/17 *b.Duisans British Cemetery, Etrun, France* — 42

Crick Pte Arthur, Suffolk Regiment (32) d.10/5/15 *b.Boulogne Eastern Cemetery, France* — 12

Cross Pte Ernest William, Royal Fusiliers (26) d.13/11/16 *No known grave, Thiepval Memorial, Somme* — 43

Cross, Pte George, Suffolk Regiment d.17/12/18 *b.Chambieres French National Cemetery, Metz, France*

Crossley Pte Charles Illingworth, Lincolnshire Regiment d.1/12/17 *No known grave, Tyne Cot Memorial, near Ypres.* — 61

Currie Lance Corporal Thomas Edward, Seaforth Highlanders (19) d.23/7/18 *No known grave, Soissons Memorial, France* — 68

Cutmore Sapper William, Royal Engineers d. 28/6/17 *b. Dozinghem Military Cem. Belgium* — 61

Dale, Lance Corporal Cyril, Royal Inniskilling Fusiliers (20) d.16/8/17 *No known grave, Tyne Cot Memorial, near Ypres* — 56

Daniels Pte Frederick James, Essex Regiment d.12/8/18 *b.Mont-Bernanchon British Cemetery, France* — 69

Daniels Sgt Harry William, Army Service Corps d.5/10/18 *b.Kantara War Memorial Cemetery, Egypt* — 69

Davey Pte William, Suffolk Regiment (25) d.18/9/15 *b.Gunners Farm Military Cemetery, Belgium.* — 12

	page
Deaves Pte William Maurice, Bedfordshire Regiment (18) d.23/10/18 b.Highland Cemetery, Le Cateau, France	65
Debenham Pte Herbert, Royal Sussex Regiment (18) d.13/8/18 No known grave, Vis-En-Artois Memorial, France	65
Dixon VD Major Robert Harrison, Army Service Corps (60) d.16/11/15 b.Pieta Military Cemetery, Malta	23
Durrant Pte George William, The Buffs (East Kent Regiment) (21) d.8/7/16 b St. Sever Cemetery, Rouen, France	43
Edey Pte Alfred, Royal Fusiliers (33) d.13/4/16 No known grave, Loos Memorial, France	
Edwards Pte William, Suffolk Regiment d.12/8/16 b Wimereux Communal Cemetery, France	
Elmer Pte Arthur John, Middlesex Regiment d.16/8/17 No known grave, Tyne Cot Memorial, near Ypres	56
Farrance Pte Alexander John, Suffolk Regiment d.13/11/16 b.Queens Cemetery, Puisieux, Somme	56
Farrance Pte Reginald Charles, East Surrey Regiment d.10/10/17 b.Hooge Crater Cemetery, near Ypres	56
Farrant Pte Harry James, Suffolk Regiment (21) d.25/8/15 No known grave, Helles Memorial, Turkey	
Felton Pte Bertie Charles, Suffolk Regiment d.11/10/18 b Deir El Belah War Cemetery, Israel	
Felton Pte Frederick William, Suffolk Regiment d.29/12/14 b.Bailleul Communal Cemetery, France	
Felton Lance Sgt Isaac, Royal Marine Light Infantry d.31/5/16 No known grave, Portsmouth Naval Memorial, Hampshire	37
Fish Drummer Edward Charles, Suffolk Regiment (29) d.28/9/17 b.Wimereux Communal Cemetery, France	44
Ford, Pte Roland, Middlesex Regiment d.17/10/17 No known grave, Tyne Cot Memorial, near Ypres	
Foster Pte Lionel, Australian Imperial Force (33) d.8/5/15 No known grave, Helles Memorial, Turkey	26
Francis Pte Clarence Cecil, Bedfordshire Regiment (19) d.17/5/18 b.Sudbury Cemetery	16
Francis DCM Pte Clement Reginald, Suffolk Regiment (22) d.16/12/14 No known grave, Menin Gate Memorial, Ypres.	6
French, Pte Arthur William, Suffolk Regiment (26) d.8/5/15 No known grave, Menin Gate Memorial, Ypres	12
French Pte James Leonard, Suffolk Regiment unable to trace record at present time	
French DCM CSM John James, Suffolk Regiment (48) d.5/1/19 b.Cairo War Memorial Cemetery, Egypt	73
Garwood Pte Stanley, Gloucestershire Regiment (19) d.21/8/17 b.Mendingham Military Cemetery, Belgium	
Gibbons Pte Henry William, Norfolk Regiment (22) d.15/9/16 b.Guillemont Road Cemetery, Somme	46
Golding Pte Alfred, Suffolk Regiment d.4/5/15 No known grave, Menin Gate Memorial, Ypres	12
Golding Pte Arthur, Royal Fusiliers d.4/12/17 No known grave, Cambrai Memorial, Louverval, France	
Golding Pte John, Suffolk Regiment d.10/4/17 No known grave, Arras Memorial, France	
Goodfellow Corporal Frederick Charles, Welsh Regiment (26) d.3/9/18 No known grave, Vis-En-Artois Memorial, France	
Goodwin, Pte Harry, Worcestershire Regiment (33) d.19/10/17 b.Outtersteene Communal Cemetery, Bailleul, France	
Goody Pte Charles Robert, Suffolk Regiment d.20/7/16 No known grave, Thiepval Memorial, Somme	43
Gould Pte Henry James, Cambridgeshire Regiment d.2/11/17 b.Hooge Crater Cemetery, near Ypres	54
Green Lance Corporal William Frank, Royal Fusiliers (18) d.21/9/18 b.Epehy Wood Farm Cemetery, Somme	65
Griggs Pte Sidney Albert, The Queen's (Royal West Surrey Regt) (20) d.29/7/18 b.Raperie British Cemetery, France	
Grimwood Pte Cyril John, Lancashire Fusiliers (19) d.1/6/18 b.Martinsart British Cemetery, Somme	
Grimwood Colour Sgt John William, Suffolk Regiment d.11/10/15 b.Chocques Military Cemetery, France	
Hagger Pte Frank Arthur, Middlesex Regiment (20) d.3/5/17 No known grave, Arras Memorial, France	74
Halestrap Driver Harry Charles, Royal Field Artillery (28) d.8/10/18 b.Flesquieres Hill British Cemetery, France	
Hammond Pte Robert James, Leicestershire Regiment (33) d.5/12/17 b. Ribecourt British Cemetery, France	55

	page
Harrison Pte Ernest George, Royal Fusiliers (36) d.17/2/17 b.Regina Trench Cemetery, Somme	60
Harrison Pte Frank, Suffolk Regiment (29) d.2/11/17 b.Gaza War Cemetery, Israel	60
Harrison Pte Frederick William, Royal Fusiliers unable to trace record at present time	
Hartley Pte Alfred Ambrose, Cheshire Regiment (31) d.19/5/21 b.Sudbury Cemetery	
Hartley Pte William, Royal Welsh Fusiliers (32) d.26/6/18 b.Karasouli Military Cemetery, Greece	
Harvey Pte William Victor, The King's (Liverpool Regiment) (27) d.23/7/17 b.Vlamertinghe New Military Cemetery, Belgium	
Hayward Sgt Alfred Ernest, Machine Gun Corps d.24/4/18 No known grave, Pozieres Memorial, Somme	
Heard Gunner Harry, Royal Field Artillery d.7/6/17 b.Brandhoek Military Cemetery, Belgium	
Hempstead Gunner Maurice J. Walter, Royal Garrison Artillery (19) d.1/5/18 b.Lapugnoy Military Cemetery, France	62
Hills, Rifleman Alfred, London Regiment (24) d.15/9/16 No known grave, Thiepval Memorial, Somme	46
Hills, Sgt Edward, Suffolk Regiment (19) d.23/4/17 No known grave, Arras Memorial, France	68
Hollingsworth Pte Percy Harold, Suffolk Regiment d.25/8/16 b.Auchonvillers Military Cemetery, Somme	42
Holt Sapper Charles George, Royal Engineers (29) d.31/1/17 b.Hammersmith Old Cemetery, London	
Hopes Pte Frank, Suffolk Regiment (21) d.27/11/17 b.Ramleh War Cemetery, Israel	
Hostler Driver Leonard, Army Service Corps (25) d.27/3/16 b.Behencourt Churchyard, Somme	
Hume Rifleman James William, Rifle Brigade unable to trace record at present time	
Hume Pte Percy, Suffolk Regiment (21) d.14/9/15 b Pieta Military Cemetery, Malta	74
Hunt CSM Wilfred Samuel, Suffolk Regiment (37) d.18/9/15 b.Hill 60 Cemetery, Turkey	22
Hurst Pte Fergus O'Connor, Northumberland Fusiliers d.16/6/17 No known grave, Arras Memorial, France	
Jarmyn Corporal Arthur A, Cameronians (Scottish Rifles) d.21/7/16 b. Albert Communal Cemetery Extension, Somme	27
Jay Lance Corporal John Francis, Suffolk Regiment (23) d.19/9/18 b Ramleh War Cemetery, Israel	69
Jennings Pte Wilfred Argent, Australian Imperial Force d.26/4/16 b.Brisbane General Cemetery, Australia	25
Joy Pte Robert Sizer, Australian Imperial Force (44) d.25/4/15 b.Lone Pine Cemetery, Anzac, Turkey.	25
Jukes Lieutenant Arthur Starr, London Regiment (44) d.6/3/17 b.Suez War Memorial Cemetery, Egypt	
Keeble Pte Frederick, Suffolk Regiment (22) d.2/11/17 b Gaza War Cemetery, Israel	60
Kemp Pte Walter William, Suffolk Regiment unable to trace record at present time	
King Pte Harry, Norfolk Regiment d.2/2/17 b.Baghdad (North Gate) War Cemetery, Iraq	
Lee Lance Corporal William Charles, Suffolk Regiment (23) d.10/10/16 No known grave, Thiepval Memorial, Somme	47
Leonard Pte James, Suffolk Regiment (21) d.7/7/17 b.Sudbury Cemetery	16
Letchford Pte Gerald, Canterbury Regiment (New Zealand) d.8/8/17 No known grave, Messines Ridge (NZ) Memorial, Belgium	
Lever Pte Ernest Edward, Northumberland Fusiliers (20) d.3/11/18 as PoW. b.Niederzwehren Cemetery, Germany	71
Locke Pte Percy William, Suffolk Regiment d.19/4/18 b.Suffolk Cemetery, La Rolanderie Farm, France	
Lorking Sgt Bertie Edwin, Machine Gun Corps (24) d.21/10/18 b Alexandria (Hadra) War Memorial Cemetery, Egypt	69
Lorkings Lance Corporal Harry, Suffolk Regiment d.24/4/15 b.Dochy Farm New British Cemetery, Belgium	12
Lumley Sgt Percy William, King's Own (Royal Lancaster Regt) (22) d.24/5/15 No known grave, Menin Gate, Ypres	
Malyon Pte Bert, Suffolk Regiment (24) d.12/3/15 b.Lille Southern Cemetery, France	40
Malyon Lance Corporal Harry Edward, East Surrey Regiment d.1/7/16 No known grave, Thiepval Memorial, Somme	38

Martin Pte Arthur George, Suffolk Regiment (40) d.28/10/17
b.Sudbury Cemetery

Martin Pte Basil James, Middlesex Regiment (24) d.23/4/17   68
b St. Nicolas British Cemetery, France

Martin Pte Bertie, Suffolk Regiment d.21/8/15 No known grave,
Helles Memorial, Turkey

Mathew Pte Charles, Royal Fusiliers d.29/3/17 b.Faubourg
D'Amiens Cemetery, Arras, France

Matthews Corporal William Charles, Machine Gun Corps   43
d.24/8/16 No known grave, Thiepval Memorial, Somme

Mattingly Pte Bernard, Canadian Infantry (28) d.29/4/17   26
No known grave, Vimy Memorial, France

Mauldon Lance Corporal George Frederick Christie Suffolk   60
Regiment, (25) d.6/11/17 b.Beersheba War Cemetery, Israel

Mayes Pte Percy John, Manchester Regiment (28) d.9/10/18
No known grave, Vis-En-Artois Memorial, France

Mixer Rifleman Frank, King's Royal Rifle Corps d.15/2/15
No known grave, Menin Gate Memorial, Ypres

Moore Pte Robert, East Kent Regiment (22) d.22/9/18   64
No known grave, Vis-en-Artois Memorial, France

Morgan Lance Sgt Ernest, Suffolk Regiment d.23/11/17
No known grave, Tyne Cot Memorial, near Ypres

Moulton Pte James William, Suffolk Regiment (27) d.9/8/17
No known grave, Arras Memorial, France

Mumford Able Seaman Harry, Royal Navy (21) d.22/9/14   7
No known grave, Chatham Naval Memorial, Kent

Mumford Pte James, London Regiment d.13/6/17
No known grave, Menin Gate Memorial, Ypres

Newman Rifleman Albert Percy, Rifle Brigade (19) d.17/8/17   56
No known grave, Tyne Cot Memorial, near Ypres

Nice Driver Jeremiah Edward, Royal Field Artillery d.14/5/16
b.Vermelles British Cemetery, France

Norman, Pte Maurice, Queen's Own (Royal West Kent Regt)
d.1/6/17 No known grave, Arras Memorial, France

Nunn Pte Robert, Suffolk Regiment d.16/9/16 No known grave,   46
Thiepval Memorial, Somme

Nunn Pte Sidney Robert, The Queen's (Royal West Surrey Regt)
(18) d.21/9/18 b.Meath Cemetery, France

Nunn Pte Stanley Percy, Suffolk Regiment (24) d.19/9/18   69
b.Ramleh War Cemetery, Israel

Parish Pte James Frederick Austin, Suffolk Regiment (19)   70
d.25/12/17 b.Sudbury Cemetery

Parker Pte George William Hyde, Suffolk Regiment d.16/11/16   41
b.Bertrancourt Military Cemetery, Somme.

Parker Pte John Edward, Essex Regiment d.23/8/18 b.Albert   65
Communal Cemetery Extension, Somme

Partridge MM Pte Percy, Suffolk Regiment (33) d.12/4/18   62
b.Suffolk Cemetery, La Rolanderie Farm, France

Partridge Pte Percy Herbert, Suffolk Regiment d.16/8/16   41
No known grave, Thiepval Memorial, Somme

Patrick Pte Walter William, Scots Guards d.5/8/17
No known grave, Menin Gate Memorial, Ypres

Pearson Corporal William, Bedfordshire Regiment (28)
d.17/5/15 b.Guards Cemetery, Windy Corner, Cuinchy, France

Pettit Sgt David William, Suffolk Regiment (23) d.8/10/15   23
b.Alexandria (Chatby) Military Cemetery, Egypt

Pettitt Able Seaman John Edward, Royal Navy (19) d.31/8/19   73
No known grave, Chatham Naval Memorial, Kent

Poole, Pte Charles Edgar, London Regiment d.14/9/16   44
No known grave, Thiepval Memorial, Somme

Poole Pte Leonard Joseph, The Buffs (East Kent Regt) (18)
d.24/8/18 b.Daours Communal Cemetery, Somme

Portfleet Pte Archibald Pennington, Queen's Own (Royal W Kent   65
Regt) (17) d.24/8/18 b.Meaulte Military Cemetery, Somme

Potter Pte Bertie James, Lancashire Fusiliers d.31/7/17
No known grave, Menin Gate Memorial, Ypres

Race Pte William George, Essex Regiment (19) d.23/3/15
b.Strand Military Cemetery, Comines-Warneton, Belgium

Radley Pte Bertram, Kings Liverpool Regiment (26) unable to
trace record at present time

Ratcliffe Pte Oliver Percy, Suffolk Regiment (34) d.11/3/16   67
b.Colchester Cemetery, Essex

Ratcliffe Pte Percy, East Yorkshire Regiment d.25/4/18
No known grave, Tyne Cot Memorial, near Ypres

Raymond Rifleman John Joseph, King's Royal Rifle Corps (22)
d.31/7/17 b Voormezeele Enclosure No.3, Ypres

Rayner Pte Owen Rupert, Queen's Own (Royal West Kent Regt)
(19) d.4/5/17 b.Faubourg D'Amiens Cemetery, Arras, France

Reeder CSM Thomas Christopher, Norfolk Regiment (28)   4
d.12/10/16 No known grave, Thiepval Memorial, Somme

Risby, Lance Corporal Charles, Suffolk Regiment (25) d.18/3/17   51
as PoW. b.Hamburg Cemetery, Germany

Rose Lance Corporal Claude Charles John, Suffolk Regiment
(26) d.19/1/20 b.Sudbury Cemetery

Sage Pte George Moutell, Army Service Corps (25) d.8/5/18
b.Dar Es Salaam (Upanga Road) Cemetery, Tanzania

Salter, Pte Harry Henry William Joseph, London Regt (London
Scottish) (21) d.7/5/17 b.Tank Cemetery, Guemappe, France

Sillett Pte Leonard Albert, The Buffs (East Kent Regt) d.1/7/16   40
No known grave, Thiepval, Somme

Sillett Pte Percy, Suffolk Regiment (20) d.2/3/16   40
No known grave, Menin Gate Memorial, Ypres

Sillitoe Pte Alfred James, Essex Regiment d.21/7/17 b. Deir El
Belah War Cemetery, Israel

Sillitoe Rifleman Henry, King's Royal Rifle Corps d.15/9/16   46
No known grave, Thiepval Memorial, Somme

Smith Pte Arthur Angelo, Suffolk Regiment (26) d.27/3/18   44
No known grave, Pozieres Memorial, Somme

Smith Corporal Ernest, Army Service Corps (43) d.31/10/18   57
b Auberchicourt British Cemetery, France

Smith Pte Gilbert Claude, Suffolk Regiment (22) d.18/8/16   44
No known grave, Thiepval Memorial, Somme

Smith Pte Harry, Suffolk Regiment d.27/9/17 No known grave,   57
Tyne Cot Memorial, near Ypres

Smith Pte James Walter, Cambridgeshire Regiment d.1/4/18
b.St. Sever Cemetery Extension, Rouen, France

Smith Lance Corporal Richard Paul, Essex Regiment d.24/5/15
No known grave, Menin Gate Memorial, Ypres

Smith Lance Corporal Sidney, King's Royal Rifle Corps (30)
d.7/5/16 b.Habarcq Communal Cemetery Extension, France

Smylie Captain Robert Stewart R, Royal Scots Fusiliers (42)   40
d.14/7/16 b.Flatiron Copse Cemetery, Mametz, Somme

Sore Pte Ernest , (King's) Dragoon Guards (33) d.3/6/15   58
No known grave, Menin Gate Memorial, Ypres

Sore Pioneer Horace Charles, Royal Engineers (22) d.19/4/17   58
No known grave, Jerusalem Memorial, Israel

Spalding Sgt Charles William, Northamptonshire Regiment   68
(35) d.5/11/18 b.Mikra British Cemetery, Kalamaria, Greece

Spreckley Pte John Ralph, Bedfordshire Regiment (22)
d.28/4/17 No known grave, Arras Memorial, France

Stammers Pte Thomas, Royal Fusiliers (26) d.7/7/16   43
No known grave, Thiepval Memorial, Somme

Stearns Pte Alfred, Suffolk Regiment (28) d.19/12/15
b.Hop Store Cemetery, Ypres

Stearns Driver John Thomas, Royal Engineers (29) d.11/11/18   70
b.Douai British Cemetery, Cuincy, France

Suttle MM Lance Corporal Ambrose, London Regiment   62
d.22/8/18 b.Bray Hill British Cemetery, Bray-Sur-Somme, Somme

Tatum Pte Ernest George, Suffolk Regiment d.30/9/15
No known grave, Menin Gate Memorial, Ypres

Thompson Sgt Frederick, Suffolk Regiment (19) d.6/11/17   60
b.Beersheba War Cemetery, Israel

Tippet Major Charles Henry, Royal Dublin Fusiliers (52)   21
d.7/8/15 b.Green Hill Cemetery, Turkey

Towler Pte Bert, The Buffs (East Kent Regt) (27) d.12/10/17
b Cement House Cemetery, Langemark, Belgium

Tuffen Pte Albert Arthur, Suffolk Regiment d.27/3/17
b Gaza War Cemetery, Israel

Turner Pte Arthur James, Coldstream Guards (32) d.12/11/14   5
No known grave, Menin Gate Memorial, Ypres

Wallace Pte Harry George, Suffolk Regiment (24) d.13/2/15
b.Wimereux Communal Cemetery, France

Walker Pte John, Middlesex Regiment d.25/7/17
b.Gorre British and Indian Cemetery, France

Ward Able Seaman Walter, Royal Naval Division (36) d.17/11/17   16
b.Sudbury Cemetery

Watson Pte Leonard John, Royal Inniskilling Fusiliers d.6/9/17
b.Hermies British Cemetery, France

Watson Pte Stanley Robert, London Regiment (21) d.16/6/17
No known grave, Arras Memorial, France

Watton Sapper Fred, Royal Engineers *Unable to trace date and place of death* — 23

Webb Pte Bertie William, Royal Fusiliers d.23/8/18 *b.Achiet-Le-Grand Communal Cemetery Extension, France*

Webb Pte Leonard Arthur, London Regiment (23) d.3/10/16 — 51
b.Carnoy Military Cemetery, Somme

Webb Gunner Wallace George, Royal Field Artillery (20) — 51
d.11/10/18 *b.Abbeville Communal Cemetery Extension, Somme*

Webb Pte William, Royal Welsh Fusiliers d.6/4/18 *b.Les Baraques Military Cemetery, Sangatte, France*

Welsh Pte Peter, Argyll and Sutherland Highlanders d.20/9/18
b.Sarigol Military Cemetery, Kriston, Greece

Wheeler Pte Frank Thomas, Canadian Infantry (26) d.1/1/17 — 50
b.Ecoivres Military Cemetery, Mont-St. Eloi, France

Wheeler Pte Frederick, London Regiment (31) d.16/6/17 — 50
No known grave, Arras Memorial, France

White Pte Charles Bernard, Suffolk Regiment (19) d.27/3/18 — 62
b.Cabaret-Rouge British Cemetery, Souchez, France

White Lance Corporal Fred Charles, Essex Regiment
Unable to trace record at present time

White Pte Sidney Philip, (King's) Hussars d.5/5/16 — 33
No known grave, Basra Memorial, Iraq

Willis John, Regiment unknown. *Unable to trace record at present time*

Wright Rifleman Percy Charles, King's Royal Rifle Corps (32)
d.31/7/17 *b.Poelcapelle British Cemetery, near Ypres*

Wright Sgt Robert William, Honourable Artillery Company (27) — 47
d.30/11/16 *No known grave, Thiepval Memorial, Somme*

Yearsley, Pte John Henry, (Queen Alexandra's Own Royal)
Hussars (30) d.23/2/19 *b.Cologne Southern Cemetery, Germany*

Names not on the War Memorial

Andrewes Colonel George Lancelot, Suffolk Regiment (60)
d.17/9/16 *b.Sudbury Cemetery*

Coote Pte E P, Middlesex Regiment (38) d.21/12/18
b.Sudbury Cemetery

Manby Pte Harry, Suffolk Regiment (42) d.25/8/20
b.Sudbury Cemetery

Mesham Lieut. Robert Seymour, West African Field Force
d.19/4/18 *b.Pemba Cemetery Mozambique.*

Stevens Pte. Albert, Suffolk Regiment d.19/7/16
No known grave, Thiepval Memorial, Somme.

Westoby Second Lieut. Frank Durrant, Middlesex Regiment
(41) d.16/9/16 *b.Combles Communal Cemetery, Somme*

1939 – 1945

Alleston Able Seaman Harry Charles, Royal Navy (47) d.20/9/45
b.Sudbury Cemetery, Suffolk

Bacon Sgt Owen, Royal Air Force Volunteer Reserve (21)
d.6/5/43 *b.Nakuru North Cemetery, Kenya*

Barnes Lieut. William Allen Frederick, Royal Army Pay Corps — 97
(45) d.11/5/41 *b.Sudbury Cemetery*

Bayfield Gunner Hubert Abdell, Royal Artillery d.13/8/45 — 134
b.Klagenfurt War Cemetery, Austria

Bear Lance Corporal Albert Charles, Suffolk Regiment (24) — 128
d.22/8/45 as PoW. *b.Kanchanaburi Cemetery, Thailand.*

Bear Gunner Frank Walter, Royal Artillery (37) d.9/12/42 as PoW. — 100
b.Florence War Cemetery, Italy.

Bird Ordinary Seaman Emrys Vernon, Royal Navy (20) — 97
d.23/5/41 *No known grave, Chatham Naval Memorial, Kent*

Cahill Pte Philip Ronald, Suffolk Regiment (25) d.6/6/43 as PoW. — 128
b.Kanchanaburi War Cemetery, Thailand

Cansdale Pte Reginald George, Suffolk Regiment (25) — 98
d.15/2/42 *No known grave, Singapore Memorial, Singapore*

Cecil Pte George Harry, Suffolk Regiment, (22) d.20/8/43 as — 129
PoW *b.Kanchanaburi War Cemetery, Thailand*

Codling Pte Thomas Edward, Cambridgeshire Regiment (29) — 128
d.6/6/43 as PoW. *b.Kanchanaburi War Cemetery, Thailand*

Cole Pte Ephraim, Bedfordshire & Hertfordshire Regt (28) — 132
d.12/9/44 as PoW *No known grave, Singapore Memorial*

Cresswell Leading Aircraftman Jack, RAFVR (22) d.15/2/43 — 104
b.Sudbury Cemetery

Dean, Flying Officer Arnold Keith Michael, RAFVR (20) — 123
d.28/8/44 *b.Engelen General Cemetery, Netherlands*

Death, Pte Paul William, Essex Regiment (24) d.25/10/42
No known grave, El Alamein Memorial, Egypt.

Dove Sgt Benjamin James, RAFVR, (22) d.26/3/42 *b. Amsterdam* — 100
New Eastern Cemetery, Netherlands

Everitt Harry Charles, Civil Defence (20) d.6/9/42 — 102
b.Sudbury Cemetery

Everitt Pte Leslie Sidney, Queen's Own (Royal West Kent Regt) — 122
(24) d.28/1/44 *b.Taukkyan War Cemetery, Burma*

Fillmore DFC Flight Lieut. Eric George, RAFVR (23) d.18/2/46 — 95
b.Sudbury Cemetery

Fillmore Sgt Kenneth Marcel, RAFVR (23) d.31/7/41 — 95
b.Sudbury Cemetery

Flowerdew, Squadron Leader John Bernard, Royal Air Force — 104
d.5/5/43 *No known grave, Air Forces Memorial, Runnymede*

French Able Seaman Reginald Charles, Royal Navy (22) — 101
d.26/9/42 *No known grave, Chatham Naval Memorial, Kent*

Golding Corporal Charles Alfred, Royal Air Force (31) d.17/6/40 — 91
No known grave, Air Forces Memorial, Runnymede

Griggs Sapper Frederick Richard, Royal Engineers (22)
d.25/10/42 *b.El Alamein Cemetery, Egypt*

Heard Petty Officer Albert, Royal Navy d.6/12/44 *No known* — 101
grave, Chatham Naval Memorial, Kent

Heard Sapper Charles, Royal Engineers (20) d.2/10/44 — 102
b.Jonkerbos War Cemetery, Netherlands

Henderson Ordinary Seaman George, Royal Navy (17) — 101
d.23/10/42 *b.Point Noire European Cemetery, Congo*

Hughes Flying Officer John Douglas, RAFVR (23) d.1/2/44 — 122
b.Hanover War Cemetery, Germany

Hurst Corporal William George, Queen's Own (Royal West Kent — 122
Regt) (24) d.26/6/44 *b.Florence War Cemetery, Italy*

Johnson Bombardier Cyril James, Royal Artillery (30) d.8/5/43 — 88
b.Massicault Cemetery, Tunisia

Johnson Sgt Thomas Reginald, Royal Artillery (33) d.8/5/43 — 90
b.Massicault Cemetery, Tunisia

Lillie DFM Sgt William Gray, Royal Air Force (21) d.21/7/40 — 93
No known grave, Air Forces Memorial, Runnymede

Marshall Flying Officer John F, RAFVR (23) d.19/9/44 — 123
b.Reichswald Forest War Cemetery, Kleve, Germany

McIntyre CQMS Robert McAusland, Suffolk Regiment (33) — 129
d.19/10/43 as PoW. *b.Chungkai War Cemetery, Thailand.*

Mills Sgt Harold, RAFVR d.22/8/44 *b.Bayeux War Cemetery,* — 125
Normandy, France

Moore Able Seaman Joseph John, Royal Navy (32) d.5/12/41 — 97
No known grave, Chatham Naval Memorial, Kent

Moore Lance Corporal Robert James, Suffolk Regiment (26) — 129
d.8/11/43 as PoW. *b.Chungkai War Cemetery, Thailand*

Mulley Sgt Jack, Royal Air Force (43) d.29/8/46 *b.Sudbury*
Cemetery

Mumford Trooper Gerald Gordon, Royal Armoured Corps (21)
d.30/8/45 *b.Munster Heath War Cemetery, Germany.*

Mumford Pte Sidney Claude, Bedfordshire & Hertfordshire — 132
Regt (40) d.12/9/44 as PoW. *No known grave, Singapore Memorial*

Nunn Pte William John, Suffolk Regiment (24) d.7/2/45 as PoW. — 129
b.Sai Wan War Cemetery, Hong Kong, China

Pearce Leading Seaman Alexander George, Royal Navy (21) — 102
d.29/4/45 *No known grave, Chatham Naval Memorial, Kent*

Pepper Pte Frederick William, Durham Light Infantry (31) — 124
d.13/9/44 *b.Brussels Town Cemetery, Belgium*

Pettit Leading Aircraftman Robert William, RAFVR (23) — 134
d.12/12/45 *b.Rangoon War Cemetery, Burma*

Pilgrim, Pte James, Suffolk Regiment (25) d.1/9/43 as PoW. — 129
b.Thanbyuzayat War Cemetery, Burma

Plampin Pte Joseph Andrew The Buffs (Royal East Kent Regt)
(33) d.13/4/45 *b.Argenta Gap War Cemetery, Italy*

Reeve Gunner Sydney Edward, Royal Artillery (25) d.21/12/39
b.Sudbury Cemetery

Ridgewell Sgt Kenneth John, RAFVR (20) d.7/12/40 — 94
No known grave, El Alamein Memorial, Egypt

Risby Pte George Charles, Cambridgeshire Regiment (21) — 98
d.24/1/42 *No known grave, Singapore Memorial, Singapore*